555 SUPER FUN ACTIVITY BOOK
FOR SMART KIDS

Find the matching shadow.

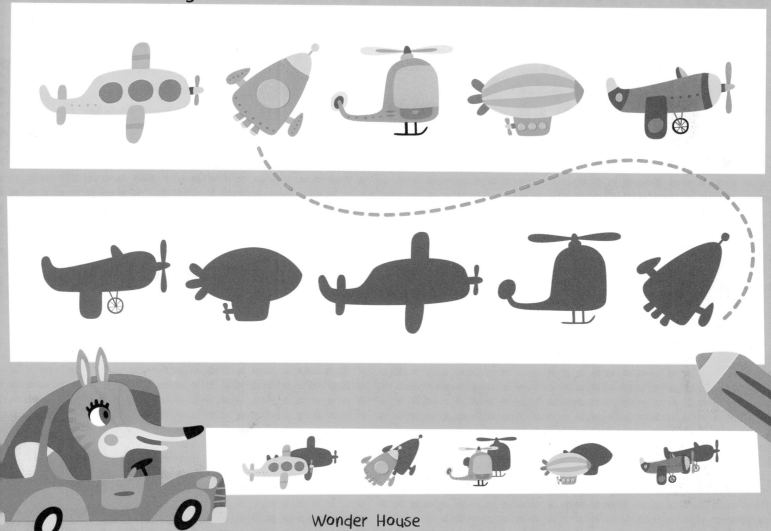

Wonder House

1. Observe the images and find the odd one out.

2. Find and match identical animals. The first one is done for you.

3. Match the animals with their shadows.

4. Connect the dots and color the picture

5. Trace and help the spiders reach their respective webs.

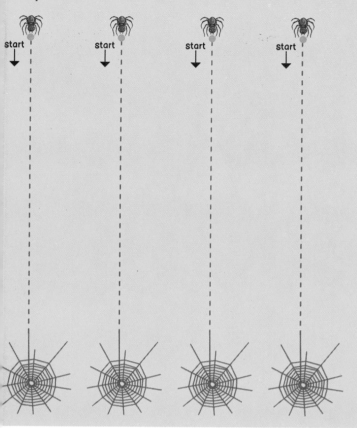

6. Trace the hot-air balloons.

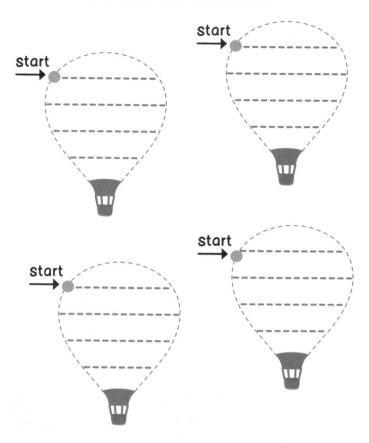

7. Trace the patterns on the fishes and color them beautifully.

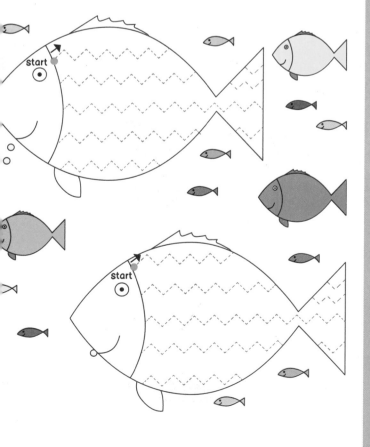

8. Help the kids hold their kites by tracing the dotted lines.

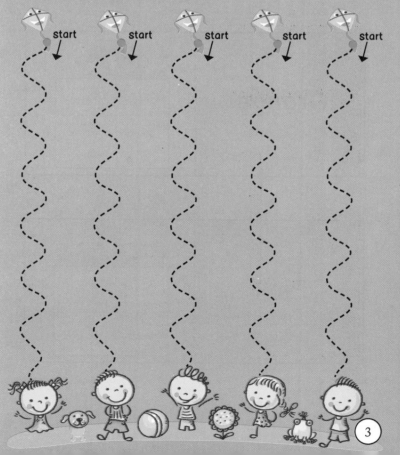

9. Identify the color written on the balloons and color them accordingly.

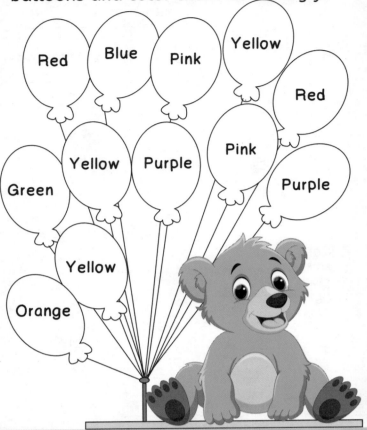

Red, Blue, Pink, Yellow, Red, Yellow, Purple, Pink, Purple, Green, Yellow, Orange

10. Circle the objects colored differently from the rest.

Red | Yellow

11. Color the gift boxes as per the color on the left.

Orange

Pink

12. Match the balloons with their missing halves.

1   2   3   4   5   6

13. Let's learn the shapes. Read them out loud.

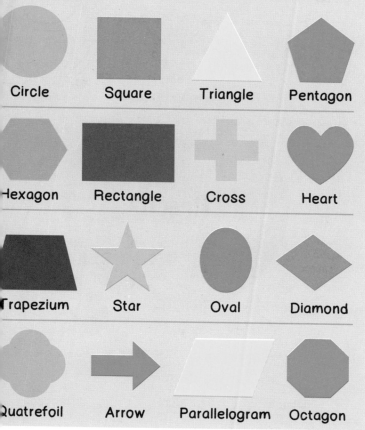

Circle Square Triangle Pentagon

Hexagon Rectangle Cross Heart

Trapezium Star Oval Diamond

Quatrefoil Arrow Parallelogram Octagon

14. Trace the dots to draw shapes. Count the number of sides in each shape and write the answer below.

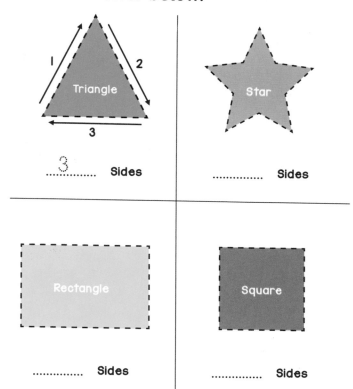

Triangle

....3.... Sides

Star

.... Sides

Rectangle

.... Sides

Square

.... Sides

15. Match the shapes.

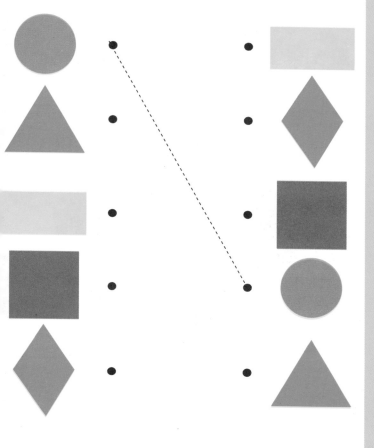

16. Build this house by correctly matching the shapes given below.

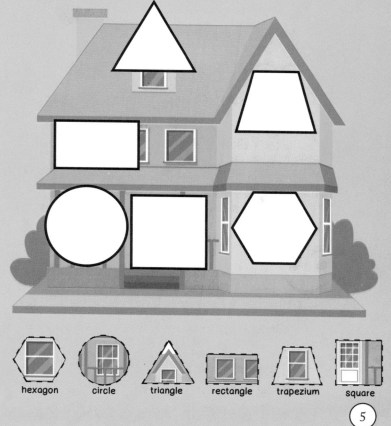

hexagon circle triangle rectangle trapezium square

17. Identify the color in the image given on the left and match it with the color given on the right.

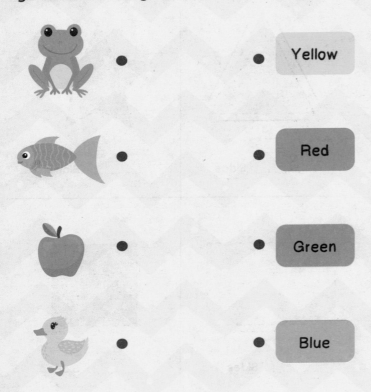

- Yellow
- Red
- Green
- Blue

18. Find the green objects and color them.

strawberry

bat

frog

tulip

Green

pea

cabbage

duck

broccoli

19. Color the caterpillar as per the color code.

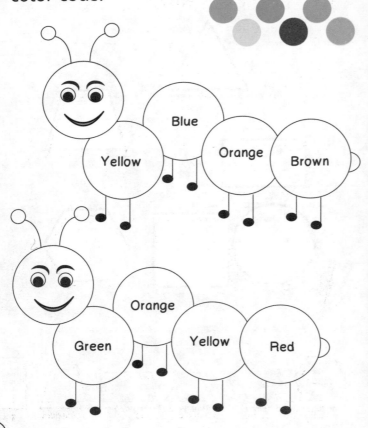

20. Circle the objects colored differently from the rest in each row.

Pink

Purple

Brown

Black

Gray

21. Complete the pattern.

22. Find and circle the odd one out.

23. Observe the shape on left. Find and color the same on right.

24. Match the objects according to their correct shapes.

25. Circle the dog that exactly matches with the one on the left.

26. Find matching socks and make pairs.

27. Find 5 differences between the two pictures.

28. Match the vehicles with their modes of transportation.

29. Help the baby monkey reach its bananas by following the path.

30. Trace the spirals to make the lollipops ready to eat!

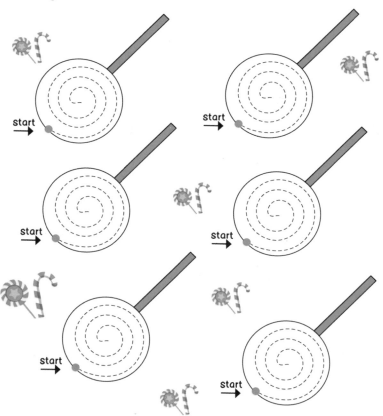

31. Complete the shells of the tortoises.

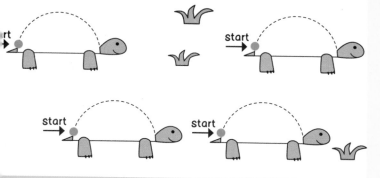

32. Help the bees reach the honeycomb by tracing their path.

33. Trace circles to complete the grapes and color them.

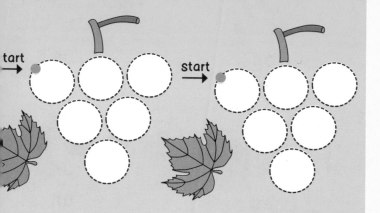

34. Trace and follow the small letters of the English alphabet to help the monkey reach his home.

35. Help the snail reach the flowers by completing the alphabet trail.

36. Connect the dots of the letter trail to get a whale and color it inside the ocean.

37. Write the missing beginning letter of each object.

.... omb

.... oor

.... og

.... us

.... ed

.... all

38. Circle the group on right that has the same number of objects as on left.

39. Trace numbers from 1-10.

40. Match the numbers with the correct number of objects.

41. What comes in the beginning?

42. Circle the group on right that has 1 more than the group on left.

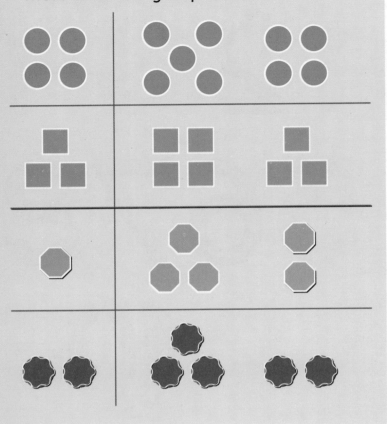

43. Use the color code at the bottom to color this basket of eggs.

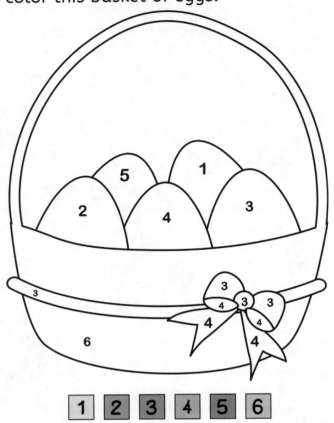

| 1 | 2 | 3 | 4 | 5 | 6 |

44. Count and write the number of cute ladybugs.

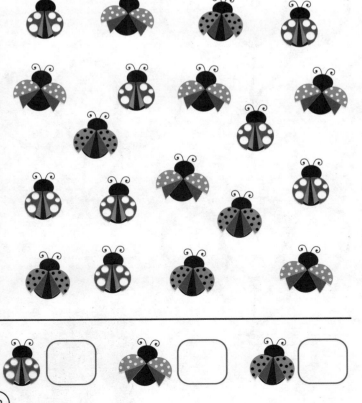

45. Count the objects given in the boxes and circle the correct answers.

| 6 | 7 | 8 | 9 | 5 |

| 2 | 8 | 3 | 6 | 10 |

12

46. Follow the letters of the English alphabet to help the dog reach his bone.

47. Color the objects with the correct small letters.

48. Circle the first letter of these objects.

K F U

V I O

N X W

A X P

B R Y

Z T U

49. Place the given letters in the correct alphabetical order.

50. Complete the pattern.

51. Circle the odd one out.

52. Find the pairs of flowers.

53. Join the dots and color the picture.

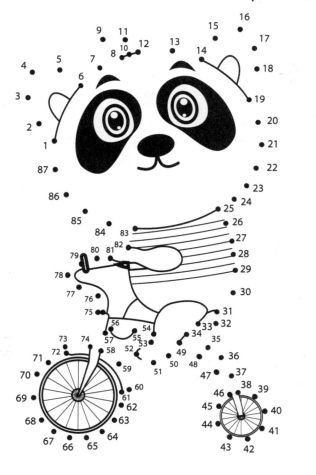

54. Trace the pattern on the hot-air balloon and color it with matching colors.

55. Spot 5 differences between the two pictures.

56. Circle the images that represent good behavior.

57. Complete the picture by identifying the missing pieces.

58. Help the racer reach the end of the maze.

59. Fill in the blank coaches with the correct capital letters and complete the alphabet train.

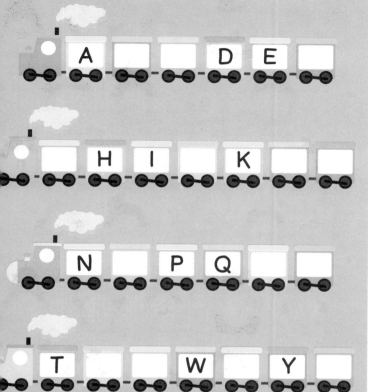

60. Match the capital letters with the fruits whose name begin with that letter.

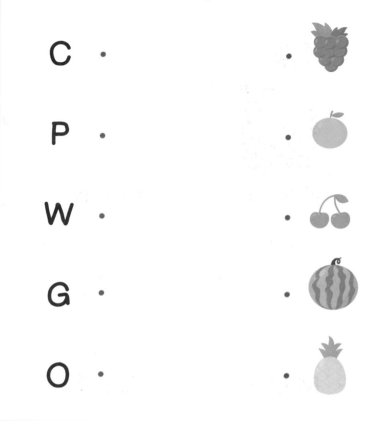

C .

P .

W .

G .

O .

61. Trace the capital letters on the left. Circle their small letters on the right.

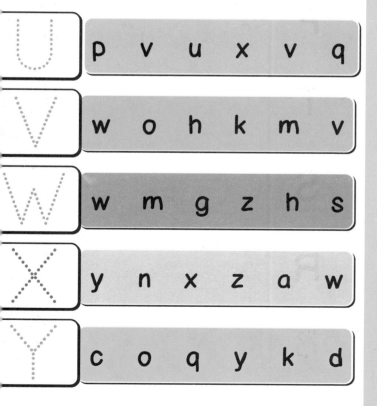

p	v	u	x	v	q
w	o	h	k	m	v
w	m	g	z	h	s
y	n	x	z	a	w
c	o	q	y	k	d

62. Fill in the blanks with the correct last letters.

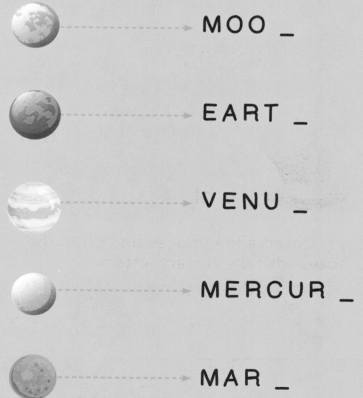

MOO _

EART _

VENU _

MERCUR _

MAR _

63. Identify the picture and circle the first letter.

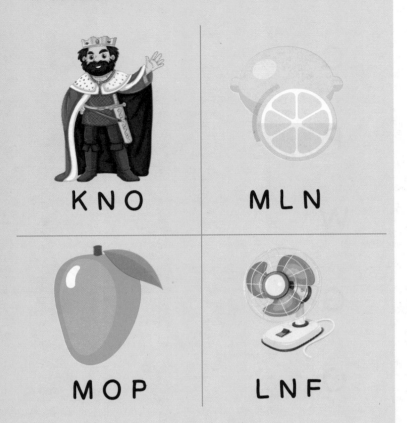

K N O   M L N

M O P   L N F

64. Fill in the missing small letters in the cupcakes to get all the alphabets.

65. Fill in the blank spaces with the right letters to make words.

.... og

.... am

.... at

66. Match the letters with the animals.

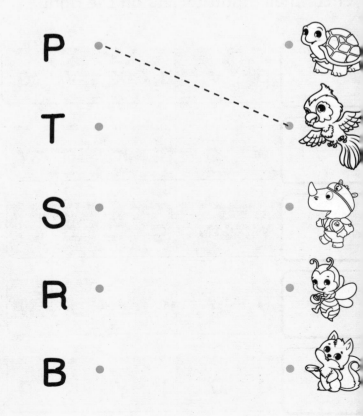

P •

T •

S •

R •

B •

67. Observe the images and fill in the boxes with the correct letters.

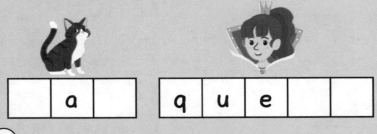

	a	

q	u	e	

68. Drive the car into the garage by color.

69. Match the circles on the left with the same color on the right.

70. Trace the lines and fill the circles with the colors of your choice.

71. Color the picture using the color code given on the left.

72. Help the hen reach the chicken through the maze.

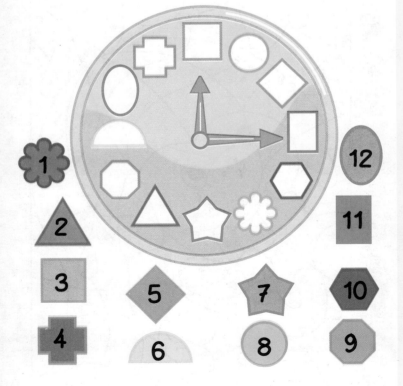

73. Guess the fruit and color it according

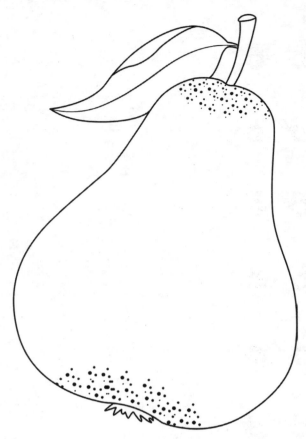

74. Complete the clock by placing the numbers in their correct positions.

75. Circle the odd one out in each row.

76. Fill in the blank spaces to complete the number sequence. Trace the circles to draw a caterpillar.

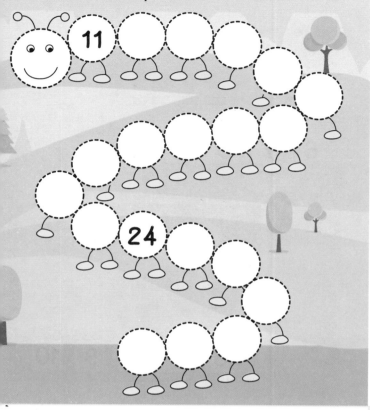

77. How many similar objects are there? Write your answer in the box provided.

78. Count the butterflies and color the correct number.

79. Count the number of muffins and write the correct number in the box.

Answer:

80. Count and write the number of animals in each box.

81. Count the gift boxes and circle the correct answer.

6 7 8 9 10

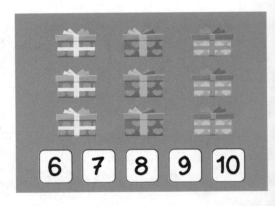

6 7 8 9 10

82. What comes in between?

12 ____ 14

4 ____ 6

17 ____ 19

9 ____ 11

5 ____ 7

18 ____ 20

83. What comes after?

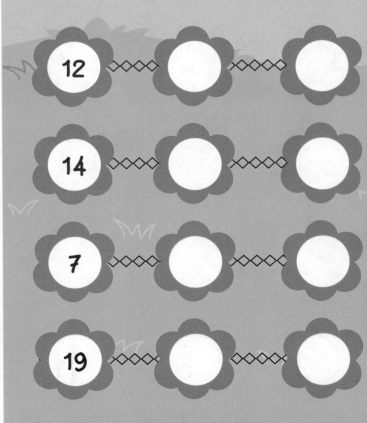

12

14

7

19

84. Can you fill the blank boxes with the right pattern?

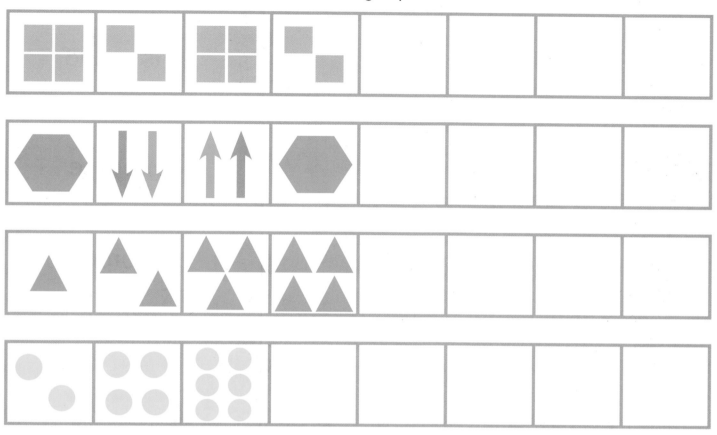

85. What will come next?

86. Fill in the blanks with the missing letters.

 _ gloo

 is _ and

 ho _ se

 mou _ e

 ice cre _ m

 _ oma _ o

 ju _ ce

 pump _ i _

87. Write the missing letter. Color the vehicle.

TAX _

88. Circle the words ending with -a, -e, -i, -o, -u. Write the words you found in the given space.

The alphabets a, e, i, o, u in the English language are known as Vowels.

Tomato Rainbow Idea Sun Frill

Kettle Media Cup Volcano Soup

Pen Banana Bottle Emu Lake

You Theatre Bonsai Piano Ski

Tea Plateau Dice Litchi Video Plain

-a	-e	-i	-o	-u

89. Choose the correct vowel.

a e i o u

a e i o u

a e i o u

a e i o u

90. How many spots do the ladybugs have?

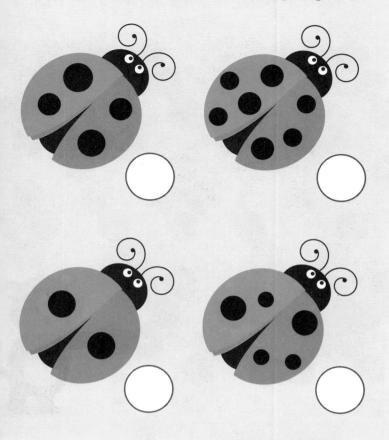

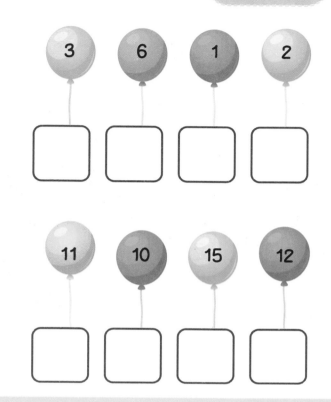

92. Place the jumbled numbers in descending order.

Descending order
Arranging numbers from largest to smallest.

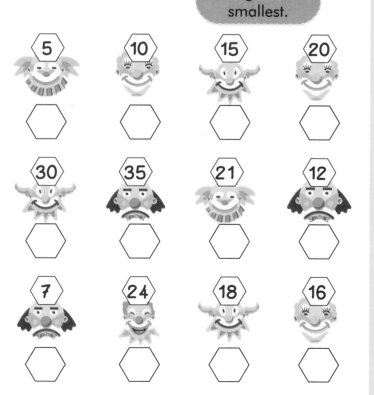

93. Write two numbers before and after the given numbers to complete the train load.

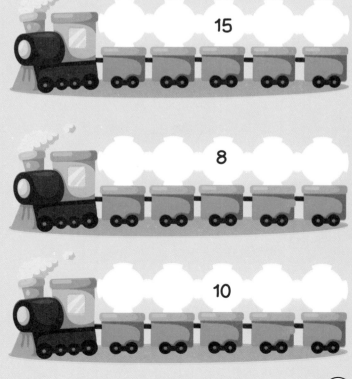

15

8

10

25

94. Can you help the bear cub reach the honey through the maze?

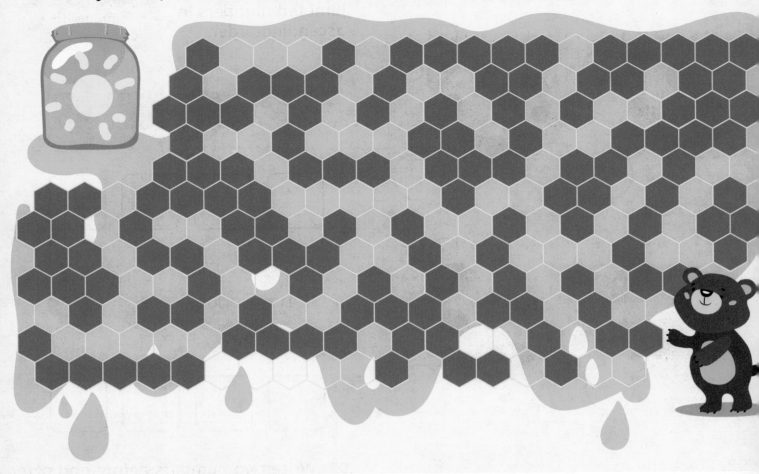

95. Complete the figure by joining the lines and color it.

96. Circle all the things wrong with the picture.

97. Study the images and replicate them in the space provided.

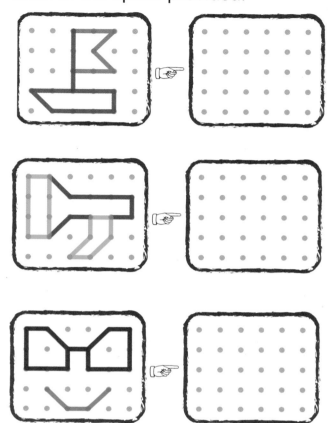

98. Find the odd one out.

December	June	July	August
October	November	April	December
Hot	Sunny	Snowy	Humid
Christmas	Ice cream	Sweater	Snowman
Leaves	Fall	Hot	Autumn
Raincoat	Water	Dry	Umbrella

99. Circle the two similar planets.

100. Write the missing numbers.

101. Match the number names with the correct numbers.

Twenty-two   40

Eleven   59

Forty   22

Fifty-nine   6

Eighty   11

Six   80

102. Round off the following numbers.

47   82   16

103   148   66

103. Use the correct sign (<, >, =).

17 •   • 98

54 •   • 32

9 •   • 99

55 •   • 55

85 •   • 102

104. Write the number names.

....

105. Name the fruits.

....

....

106. Make new words from the given ones.

TAR _____

SIGN _____

TEN _____

STAN _____

NAP _____

107. Fill the boxes with the missing vowels.

	N	G	E	L
C
O
R
N

	A	G	L	E
L
F

	N	D	E	R
N
C
L
E

	S	L	A	N	D
C
E

	C	E	A	N
T
T
E
R

	N	S	E	C	T
R
O
N

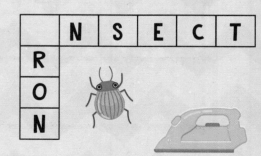

108. Find and circle the objects given below in the picture.

109. Color the picture using the color code.

red

yellow

green

brown

110. Can you circle your favorite fruits and vegetables?

111. Help the baby monkey reach the bananas.

112. Match the job and its practitioner.

113. Put (✓) on the correct shadow of each object given below.

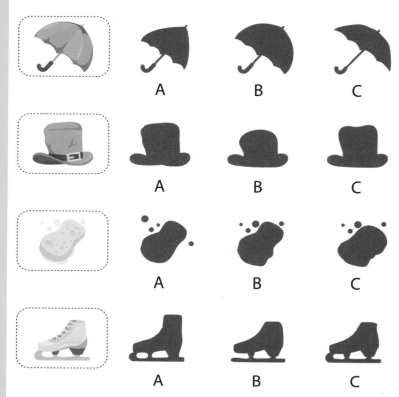

A B C

A B C

A B C

A B C

114. Trace to complete the picture. Color and name it.

_____

115. How does a butterfly grow? Number the given pictures from 1–4 in the order of the growth of a butterfly.

116. Add the leaves and write the answers.

🍂 🍂 + 🍂 = ☐

🍂 + 🍂 = ☐

🍂🍂🍂 + 🍂🍂 = ☐

🍂🍂 + 🍂🍂 = ☐

117. Add the fruits and vegetables. Write the answers in the box.

118. Add the twos.

2 + 2 + 2 + 2

+ 2 + 2 = ☐

120. Double it up!

7 + 7 = ◯

6 + 6 = ◯

8 + 8 = ◯

119. Solve the problems and color the butterfly by numbers.

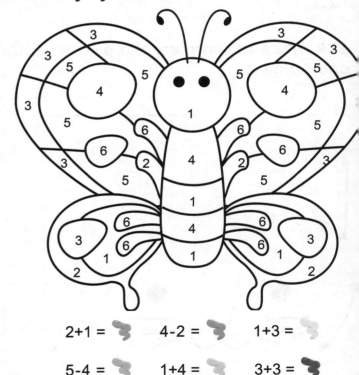

2+1 = 🐛   4-2 = 🐛   1+3 = 🐛

5-4 = 🐛   1+4 = 🐛   3+3 = 🐛

121. Color the bone that has an even answer.

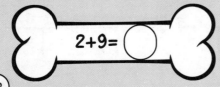

2+9= ◯

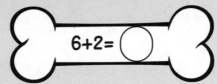

6+2= ◯

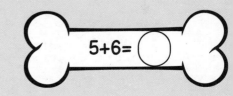

5+6= ◯

122. Subtract the given images and write the answer.

- =
- =
- =
- =

123. Count all the dinosaurs that are not crossed and circle the correct number.

| 4 | 6 | 3 | 8 |

| 1 | 3 | 5 | 2 |

124. Subtract using the number line. Draw the jumps that you make and write the answers.

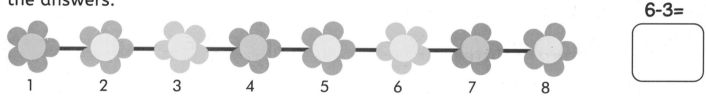

1 2 3 4 5 6 7 8

6-3=

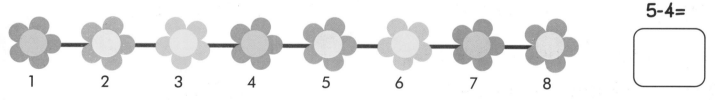

1 2 3 4 5 6 7 8

5-4=

125. Fill the missing numbers by subtracting 3 from each tomato.

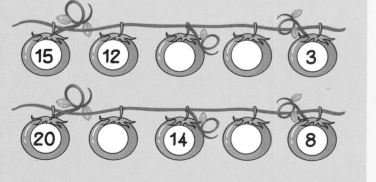

126. Find the difference and color the eggs as per the answer.

10 - 6 =

127. Read aloud the words in the grid and circle the ones you spot in the picture.

hut	bed	jug
dip	dam	log
sun	mat	top
fan	man	fig
boy	tub	cat
girl	dog	bin
web	egg	cap

128. Circle the words that begin with a consonant sound.

> All the letters in the English alphabet apart from the vowels a, e, i, o, and u are known as Consonants.

Toucan   Panda   Under   Carrot

Mango   Tiger   Otter

Orange   Igloo   Tomato   Eagle

Donkey   Ape   Ice Cream

Umbrella   Sky   Gorilla   Spoon

Love   Ink pot   Airplane

129. Look at the pictures and fill in the missing consonants to complete each word.

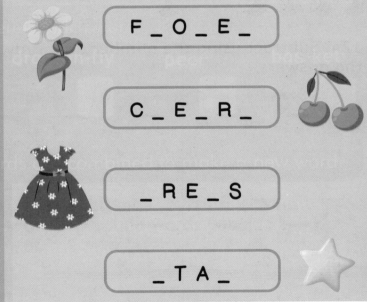

F _ O _ E _

C _ E _ R _

_ R E _ S

_ T A _

Sound blends are a set of two or three consonants that when pronounced together, retain their sound. Blends are found either at the beginning or at the end of a word.

130. Write three words for each sound blend.

br	ng	st

131. Match the blends on the left to the letters on the right to complete each word.

st •   • ider

sn •   • um

sp •   • ipt

gr •   • ail

gl •   • ork

scr •   • oves

fr •   • own

dr •   • ass

br •   • uit

132. Fill in the blanks with the correct sound blends.

1. The _ _ og came out of the water.

2. _ _ ink one glass of milk everyday.

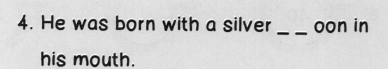

3. _ _ ush your teeth daily.

4. He was born with a silver _ _ oon in his mouth.

133. Can you write 5 words with a vowel in the middle? Say the words out loud as you write.

134. Sort the jumbled words with double letters zz, ll, ss, oo, ee, & ff. Write them in the given space.

dam, under, bee, buzz, igloo, tree, full, teeth, fluff, face, bell, toss, skull, cliff, hoop, food, puzzle, red, yak, brass, sharp, candy, touch, green, floss, staff, blizzard

zz ----------------------------------

----

ll ----------------------------------

----

ss ----------------------------------

----

oo ----------------------------------

----

ff ----------------------------------

----

ee ----------------------------------

----

135. Subtract the given numbers on the watermelon slices and write the answers.

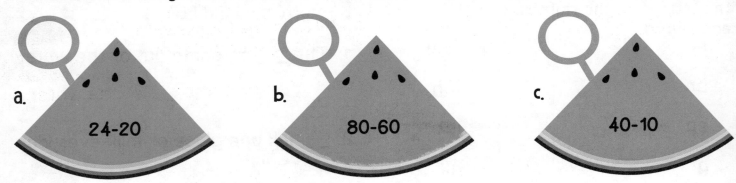

a. 24-20

b. 80-60

c. 40-10

136. Fill in the missing numbers by subtracting 2 each time.

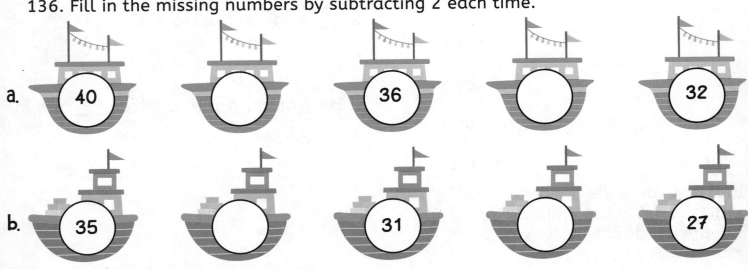

a. 40   36   32

b. 35   31   27

137. Subtract correctly to make the UFOs go away.

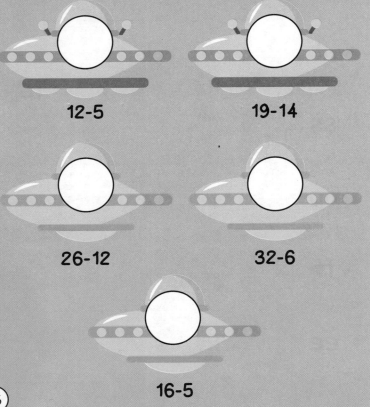

12-5

19-14

26-12

32-6

16-5

138. Solve the subtractions to get the color codes. Color the engine.

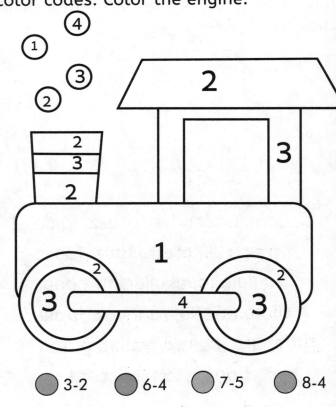

3-2   6-4   7-5   8-4

36

139. Solve the following sums.

 $=$ [ ]

 $=$ [ ]

 $=$ [ ]

 $=$ [ ]

140. Color the boxes blue if the sum is 12.

2 0	1 6	0 5
+ 4	+ 2	+ 7

[ ] [ ] [ ]

0 8	1 0	8 7
+ 4	+ 2	+ 1

[ ] [ ] [ ]

141. Add the ice cream cones and write their sums in the scoop.

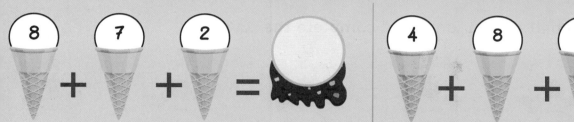

142. Solve the sums and fill in the blanks with the correct answers.

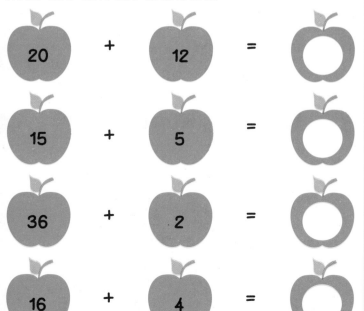

20 + 12 =

15 + 5 =

36 + 2 =

16 + 4 =

143. Put a (✓) in front of correct sums.

16 + 9 = 30 ( )

10 + 4 = 14 ( )

9 + 3 = 12 ( )

12 + 2 = 15 ( )

18 + 2 = 20 ( )

20 + 5 = 27 ( )

37

144. Help the bunny move forward by drawing the jumps on the number line.

1 + 3 =

5 + 3 =

145. Add 3 to each bell as you jump and complete the row.

6   12   21

146. Add the given images and circle the correct answer.

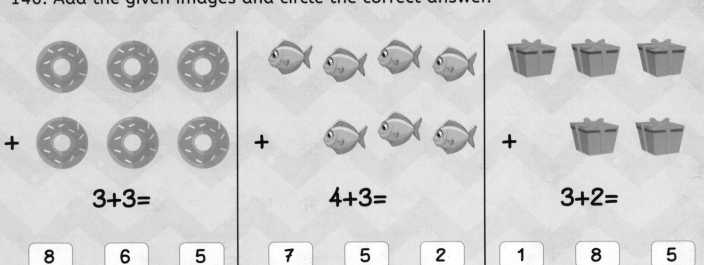

3 + 3 =

4 + 3 =

3 + 2 =

| 8 | 6 | 5 |

| 7 | 5 | 2 |

| 1 | 8 | 5 |

38

147. Count and subtract. Write the answers in the given boxes.

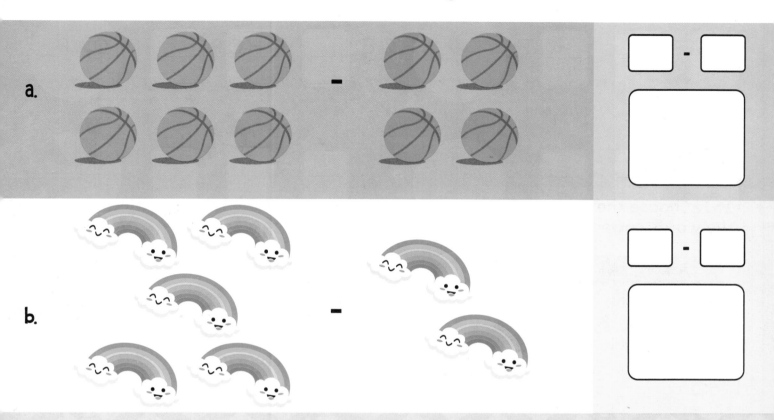

a.
☐ - ☐

☐

b.
☐ - ☐

☐

148. Subtract the given numbers and write the difference in the space provided.

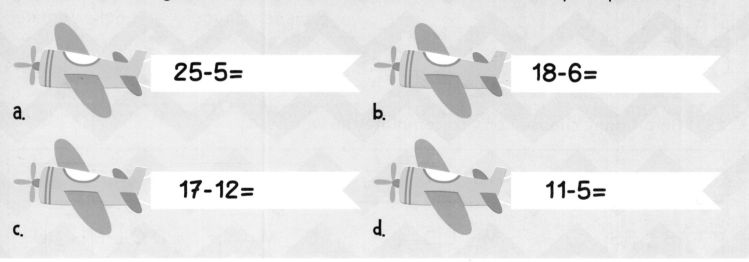

a. 25-5=

b. 18-6=

c. 17-12=

d. 11-5=

149. Subtract and write the difference in the empty circles.

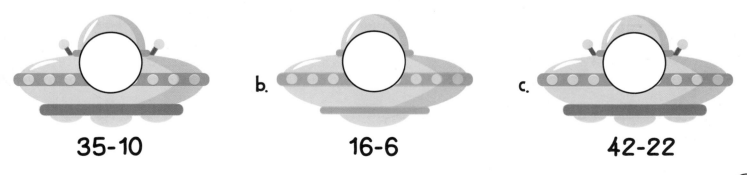

35-10

b. 16-6

c. 42-22

150. Jake is adding the letter e to his words. Can you help him? Read the words aloud before and after adding e and observe how they change.

TAP _	KIT _	ROB _	HOP _	CAP _
↓	↓	↓	↓	↓
....	....	....	....	....

151. Choose the right spellings to spell the words correctly.

AY or AI	OI or OY
T _ _ L	B _ _ L
R _ _ N	_ _ L
D _ _	T _ _
S N _ _ L	E N J _ _
H _ _	C _ _ N
V _ _ N	N _ _ S E

152. Circle the words spelled correctly.

Rhythm/Rithm	Gynger/Ginger
Piramid/Pyramid	Bicycle/Bicicle
Single/Syngel	Angel/Eangle
Eagel/Eagle	Flyeeng/Flying
Sauscer/Saucer	Locket/Lauket
Zinger/Zingre	Pleez/Please

153. Help Danny choose i or y to complete the words.

W R _ T E R	RO _ AL	P R _ M E	T _ P E
AB _ SS	M _ L D	G _ M	D O L P H _ N
S _ N K	_ ELLOW	F _ N A L	H _ PE

154. Complete the words by adding a vowel.

J _ R	R _ T	_ CE

155. Can you think of some double letter words? Say each word aloud as you write

40

156. Write two rhyming words for each in the jar.

FAN

HOLE

PLACE

COOK

157. Match the pictures with the words that rhyme. Say the words out loud.

COAT

TOAD

TREE

SOCK

TOP

FEEL

BLUE

PAIL

DIG

RACK

158. Write the word that rhymes with the word in red.

The pot is h _ t. 	There is a mouse in the _ o u _ _. 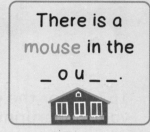
The frog jumped over the _ o _ . 	The king likes to s _ n _ . 
My coat is in the b _ _ t.	Keep the fish in the _ i s _. 

159. Identify each picture. Then, write the word and add 'e' to make a new word.

.... + E ....

.... + E ....

.... + E ....

.... + E ....

160. Tick the animal that matches its part shown on the left.

161. Tick the words that show the movement of these creatures.

walk / fly / swim

crawl / fly / swim

crawl / fly / walk

crawl / fly / swim

162. Color the given pictures using your fingerprints.

163. Color the box with the correct word for the given pictures.

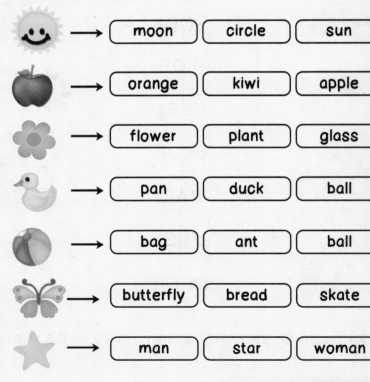

moon	circle	sun
orange	kiwi	apple
flower	plant	glass
pan	duck	ball
bag	ant	ball
butterfly	bread	skate
man	star	woman

164. How's the weather? It's

165. Is it hot today? No, it's

166. Can you guess the weather?

167. Is it windy today? No, it's

168. Circle the animals you will see on the farm.

169. Fill in the numbers that come before and after the given number.

a.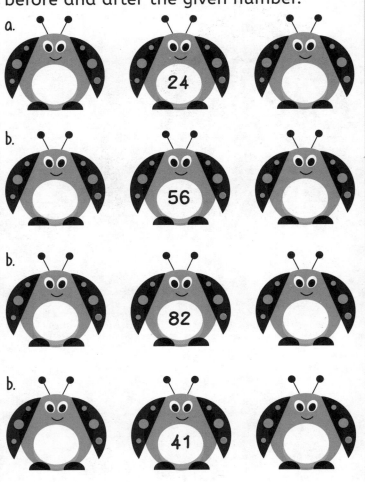

 | | 24 | |

b.

 | | 56 | |

b.

 | | 82 | |

b.

 | | 41 | |

170. 5 seeds were planted in each pot. How many still need to grow? Write the answer in the circle given.

171. Draw each bee's route to the purple flower by following the instructions.

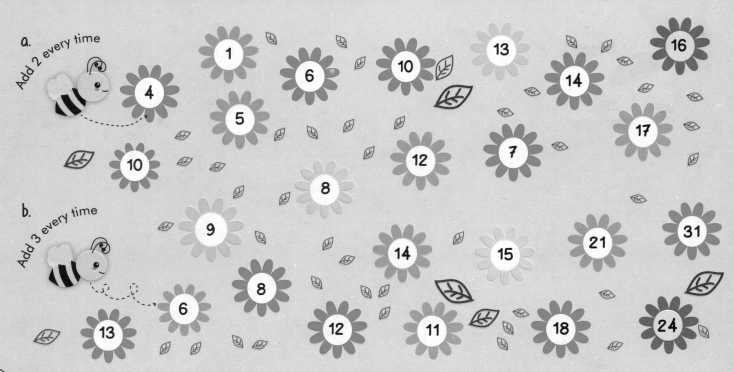

a. Add 2 every time

b. Add 3 every time

44

172. If "O" is 2, "W" is 3, and "L" is 4, what is the total of-

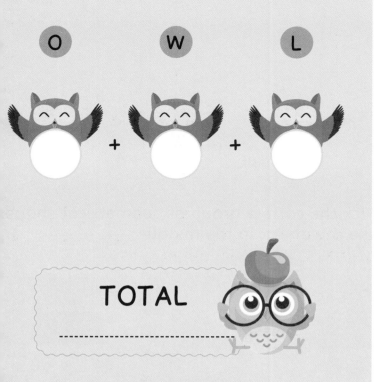

O   +   W   +   L

TOTAL
----

173. Fill in the boxes with the missing numbers between 1 & 50.

1				5
6				
11				15
		18		20
	22			

27	28	29	
32			
37	38		
			44
	48		

174. Skip count by 5 and complete the sequence.

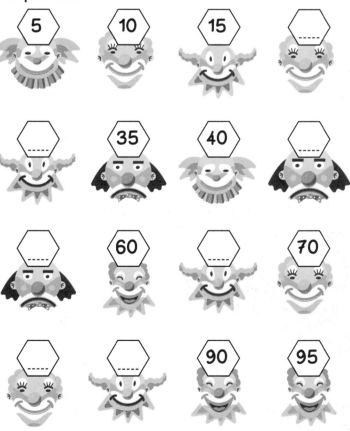

5   10   15   ____

____   35   40   ____

____   60   ____   70

____   ____   90   95

175. Skip count by 2 in reverse order and reach the end.

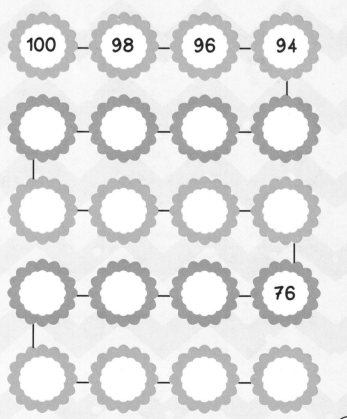

100 — 98 — 96 — 94

76

176. Complete the insect sudoku.

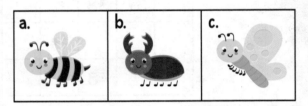

a.   b.   c.

177. Light or heavy?

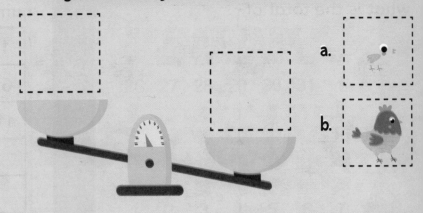

a.

b.

179. Tick the correct group of geometrical shape to make the object in the middle.

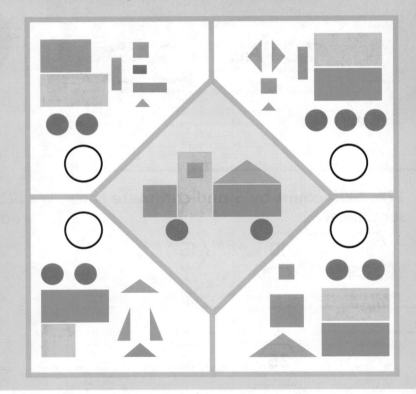

178. Write the correct order of planting.

180. Help the goat find its favorite food.

a.

b.

c.

181. Cross out the unhealthy food items.

182. Find 5 differences in the pictures given below.

183. Write plurals of the following.

Shoe	Tree	Monkey	Boy	Pen

....	....	....	....	....

184. Place these words correctly.

> Cows   Doll   Cup   Rabbits
> Dog   Chairs   Cars
> Cherry   Cake   Knives

SINGULAR

....

....

PLURAL

....

....

185. Fill in the missing letters using the picture clues.

S T R _ _ _ _ _ R R Y

U _ _ _ _ E L L _ _

N _ _ _ S _ _ _ _ E R

187. Match the rhyming words.

 •   •

 •   •

 •   •

 •   •

• •

186. Can you think of some words that rhyme with 'rain and door'?

188. Complete the sentence by writing plurals in the blanks.

One cherry. Four _____

One car. Six _____

One puppy. Two _____

One cake. Five _____

One person. Three _____

One plate. Four _____

189. Choose the correct option to describe the pictures.

Homophones are two or more words that have same pronunciation but different meanings, origins, or spellings.

Deer / Dear _____

Bare / Bear _____

Right / Write _____

190. Color the cup blue if it has a vowel under it.

K   A   P

C   I   O

Y   U   E

191. Complete the rhyme using the words from the box.

Rain	Crawled	Spider
Spout	Again	Dried

The itsy bitsy spider _____ up the water _____.

Down came the _____, and washed the spider out.

Out came the sun, and _____ up all the rain.

And the itsy bitsy _____ went up the spout _____.

192. Count the syllables in each word and then draw a line to match with the right number.

Syllable is a word or part of a word with a vowel sound formed by the opening and closing the mouth. The number of the vowel sounds in a word determines the number of syllables the word has.

Cobweb • • 4

Animal • • 1

Lunch • • 2

Caterpillar • • 3

193. Look at the pictures and unscramble the words.

 TBA _____

 NVA _____

 MPLA _____

 KSDE _____

 NMA _____

 ITKE _____

194. Let's find how many syllables are there in each word.

gar-den	horn	muf-fin	drag-on-fly	pear	bas-ket
 ☐	☐	☐	☐	☐	☐

A compound word is formed when two words are combined to make a new word.

195. Observe carefully and write the compound words in the space provided.

sun + flower = ...

star + fish = ...

blue + berry = ...

air + plane = ...

water + melon = ...

196. Challenge yourself! Write all the compound words you can think of in 2 minutes.

197. Look at the pictures and write the new word for each pair.

....

....

....

....

198. Read aloud each word and write the syllables.

Children ....

Letter ....

Movie ....

Chicken ....

Underground ....

Banana ....

Watermelon ....

Monkey ....

Chimpanzee ....

199. Underline the compound words in the given sentences. Write the words in the given space.

Rocky found a pencil near a riverbank.

.... = ... + ...

Nina eats a strawberry a day.

.... = ... + ...

Tom went to Italy in an airplane.

.... = ... + ...

Pam made a pancake for breakfast.

.... = ... + ...

A butterfly has beautiful wings.

.... = ... + ...

Mary is playing in the backyard.

.... = ... + ...

200. Draw using fingerprints.

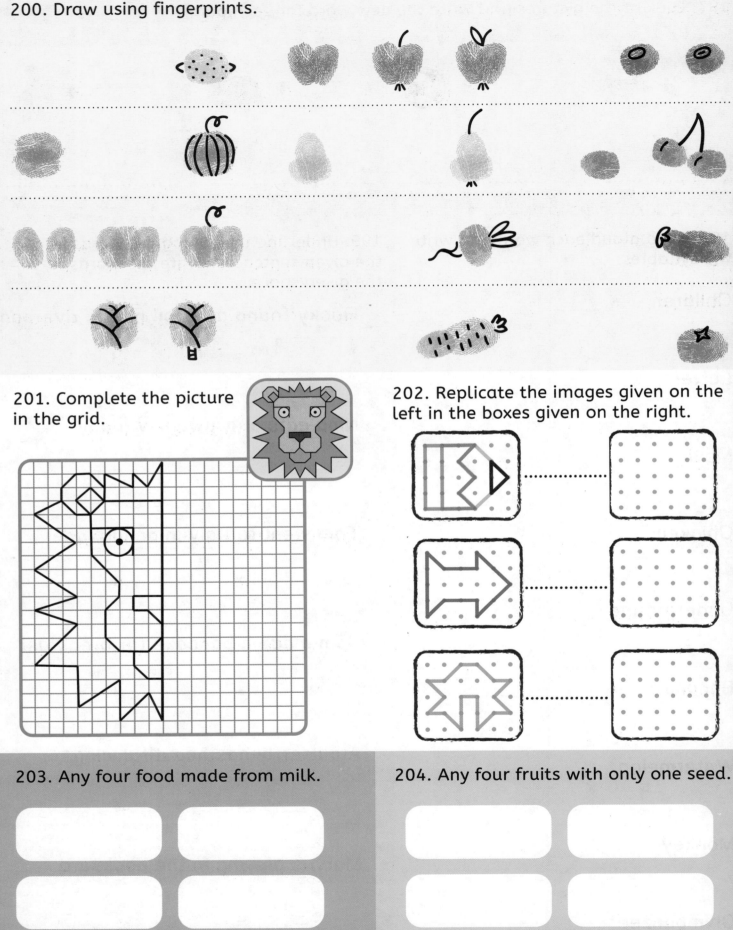

201. Complete the picture in the grid.

202. Replicate the images given on the left in the boxes given on the right.

203. Any four food made from milk.

204. Any four fruits with only one seed.

205. Is it solid, liquid, or gas?

Shampoo

Water Vapor

Syrup

Ice Cube

Cookie

Oxygen

206. Match the picture with the correct shadow.

207. Help Alex reach her house on her new scooter.

208. What's the time on the clocks?

a.

b.

c.

d.

209. Draw hands on the clocks to show the time. Write the time in figures in the boxes

a. Six o'clock   `06:00`

b. Seven o'clock

c. Twelve o'clock

d. Three o'clock

210. Show time on the clocks that the snails are carrying on their backs.

2:00

5:30

8:35

211. Help Dylan get his treats by drawing hands on the clocks.

a.

Four o'clock

b.

Quarter past nine

c.

Half past seven

d.

Quarter to one

212. Choose the correct fraction.

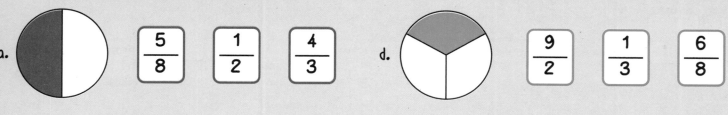

a. $\dfrac{5}{8}$ $\dfrac{1}{2}$ $\dfrac{4}{3}$

d. $\dfrac{9}{2}$ $\dfrac{1}{3}$ $\dfrac{6}{8}$

b. $\dfrac{4}{12}$ $\dfrac{13}{5}$ $\dfrac{3}{8}$

e. $\dfrac{5}{8}$ $\dfrac{5}{6}$ $\dfrac{4}{6}$

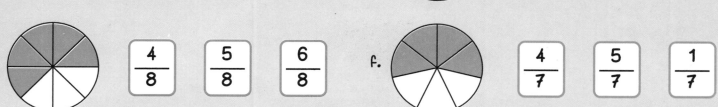

c. $\dfrac{4}{8}$ $\dfrac{5}{8}$ $\dfrac{6}{8}$

f. $\dfrac{4}{7}$ $\dfrac{5}{7}$ $\dfrac{1}{7}$

213. Color and write the fraction.

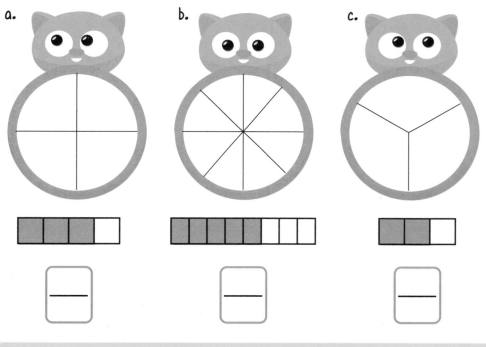

a.

b.

c.

214. Write the fraction of the colored fruit seeds.

a.

b.

215. Write fractions of the white part of the fruit.

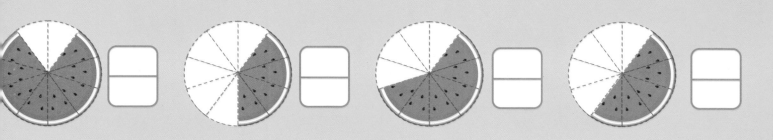

216. Measure the height and write it in the box.

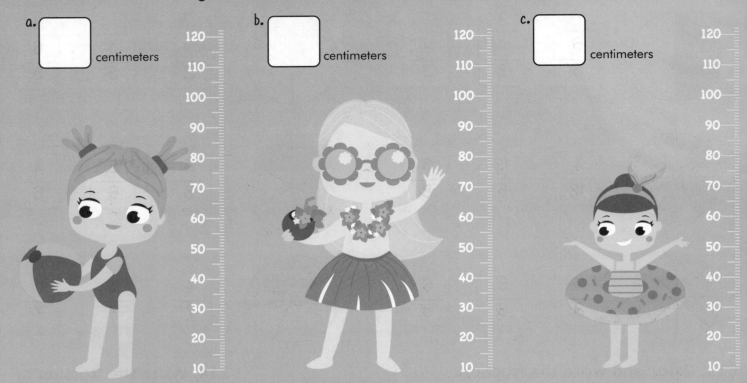

a. ☐ centimeters

b. ☐ centimeters

c. ☐ centimeters

217. If 1 feet=12 inches, convert and write.

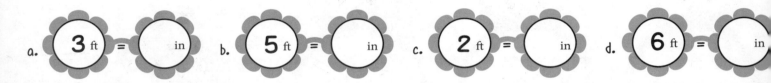

a. **3** ft = ◯ in   b. **5** ft = ◯ in   c. **2** ft = ◯ in   d. **6** ft = ◯ in

218. 1 kg=1000 g. Solve the following accordingly.

5 kg + 2 kg = ☐ g

9 kg + 400 g = ☐ g

2500 g + 100 g = ☐ g

1.5 kg + 200 g = ☐ g

3 kg + 400 g = ☐ g

7 kg + 50 g = ☐ g

219. Write the capacity.

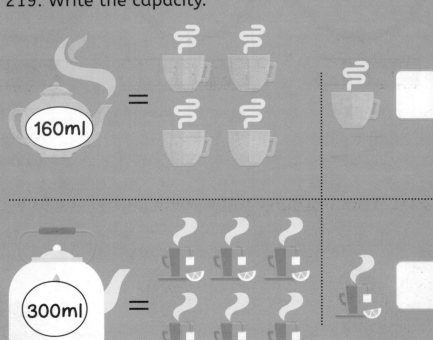

160ml = (4 cups)   ☐

300ml = (9 cups)   ☐

220. Solve the fraction sums.

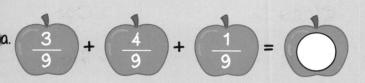

a. $\dfrac{3}{9} + \dfrac{4}{9} + \dfrac{1}{9} = \bigcirc$

b. $\dfrac{1}{5} + \dfrac{1}{5} + \dfrac{2}{5} = \bigcirc$

c. $\dfrac{3}{7} + \dfrac{1}{7} + \dfrac{2}{7} = \bigcirc$

221. a. There are 10 skirts on the rack. Gilly took 3. What fraction of the skirts did she take?

221. b. Jane saw 7 starfish and brought 2 home with her. What fraction of the starfish did she bring home?

222. Color the fruits according to the given fractions.

$\dfrac{5}{7}$

$\dfrac{2}{5}$

223. Solve the fractions and color the rings accordingly.

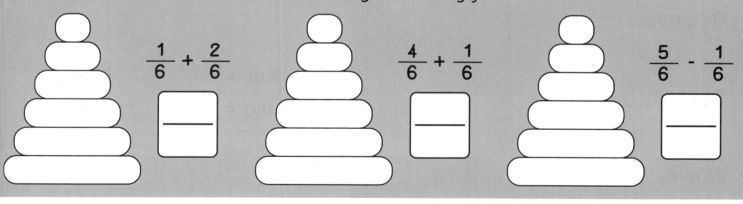

$\dfrac{1}{6} + \dfrac{2}{6}$

$\dfrac{4}{6} + \dfrac{1}{6}$

$\dfrac{5}{6} - \dfrac{1}{6}$

224. Compare the fractions and mark greater than or less than (<, >).

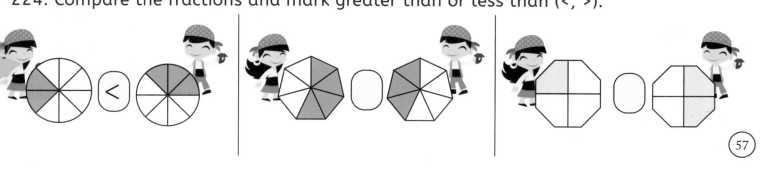

225. Write 3 singular words that you can think of and then write their plurals in the baskets.

Singular

Plural

226. Match the rhyming pairs.

Class • • Cat

Night • • Floor

Bat • • Bake

Door • • Grass

Face • • Flight

Cake • • Chase

227. Count and write the syllables in each word.

Tuna .... ☐

Seal .... ☐

Fish .... ☐

Octopus .... ☐

Oyster .... ☐

Whale .... ☐

Dolphin .... ☐

Shrimp .... ☐

228. Complete the word sums to make new words.

Rattle + snake =

....

Arm + chair =

....

Base + ball =

....

Rain + coat =

....

Ear + ring =

....

Skate + board =

....

Body + guard =

....

Lap + top =

....

229. Read the sentence aloud. Can you count and write the vowels and consonants in this sentence?

Aly is a cute girl.

Vowels:

Consonants:

231. Fill in the missing blends to complete each word and sentence.

Pam _ _ ives the car slowly.

Aliens travel in a _ _ aceship.

Buildings are made of _ _ icks

Mike used _ _ ayons for coloring.

232. Look at the picture and fill in the missing letters. Then, put a '/' to separate each syllable in the word.

_ r a _ g _

230. Add s or es to the words and turn these into plurals.

Feather + ... = ...

Boy + ... = ...

Animal + ... = ...

Bus + ... = ...

Zoo + ... = ...

Match + ... = ...

House + ... = ...

Pencil + ... = ...

Brush + ... = ...

Carrot + ... = ...

233. Can you put these things in the right box?

cup, books, bag, scissor, shells, cake, bat, balloons, necklace

Singular

Plural

234. Choose the correct word to complete the sentences.

| Orange | Fish | Books | Home |

A _____ can swim.

The _____ is sweet.

This is my _____.

I like to read _____.

235. Complete the sentences using 'a' and 'an'.

We are going for _____ movie.

I ate _____ orange for breakfast.

Can I borrow _____ pencil?

It's _____ beautiful day!

Could you get me _____ ice cream

236. Rewrite the jumbled sentences.

is my cat This.

_____

fun Reading a activity is.

_____

won quiz Jake the.

_____

pants blue The made are of cotton.

_____

237. Place the words next to the correct animal.

| Grass | Loyal | Bone |
| Neigh | Hoofs | Paws |

....

....

....

....

....

238. I have a trunk and two tusks. I am huge. Who am I?

_____

239. I have gills and scales. I swim in water. Who am I?

_____

240. How many animals can you name for each category?

SEA ANIMALS	WILD ANIMALS	FARM ANIMALS

241. Add the vowel 'a' and write the words below.

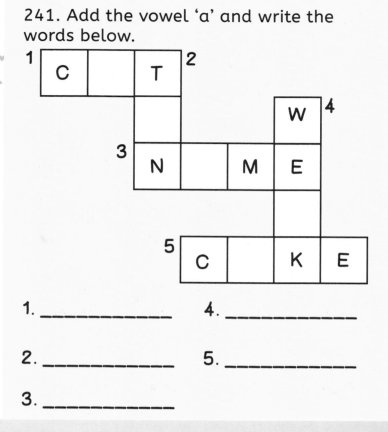

1. _____   4. _____

2. _____   5. _____

3. _____

242. Join the given words to make one word.

Butter + Cup	Egg + Shell	Basket + Ball	Flower + Bed	Rain + Bow

243. Pick the correct synonyms of the given words.

Pretty Cheerful Unattractive Make Big

Ugly

Beautiful

Create

Huge

Happy

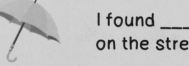

244. Fill in the blanks with 'a', 'an', or 'the'.

_____ car is damaged.

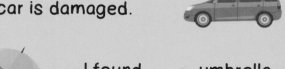

 I found _____ umbrella on the street.

Can I borrow _____ safety pin?

 _____ airplane is flying in the sky.

245. Circle the odd one in each row.

Laptop	Mouse	Cat	Keyboard
Apple	Orange	Cherry	Capsicum
Cup	Notebook	Plate	Spoon
Pencil	Crayon	Pen	Book
Pizza	Tea	Milk	Coffee

246. Check the calender.

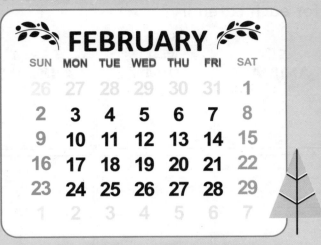

How many days were there in February 2020?

_____

What day of the week was 10ᵗʰ February?

_____

247. Color the owl using fingerprint patterns.

248. Can you name the body parts.

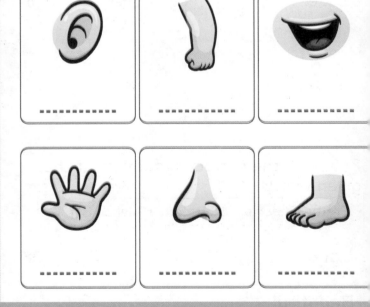

249. Look at the pictures and identify the planets.

250. What are the shapes of the given objects?

251. Match the words with the images.

Towel

Sunglasses

Hat

Beach Umbrella

Flip-Flops

Swimsuit

Sandcastle

Bucket

Shovel

Beach Ball

Sunscreen

252. Where do you keep the following items?

Where are the toothbrushes?

Where is the television?

Where are the pillows?

Where is the sofa?

Where is the bed?

----

253. Mark the vehicles you have traveled in.

254. Match the animals with their shadows.

255. Observe and match the boy's different expressions.

Lying

Sulking

Thinking

Happy

256. Help the school bus driver find his way to the school.

257. Match the emotions with the correct expressions.

Sad

Happy

Angry

Surprised

258. Observe the emotions and choose the odd one out.

259. Write 'H' in front of healthy food and 'UH' in front of unhealthy food.

Watermelon   Burger   Cold Drink

Juice   Broccoli   Soup

260. Write (P) for plant-based and (A) for animal-based food.

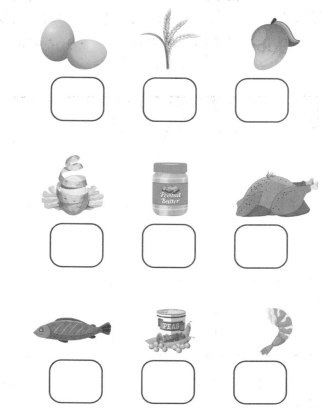

261. Who Am I?

Green on the outside, red on the inside. So many seeds; what to do you decide.

_____

Yellow in color and tastes sour, Refreshing summer drink for each hour.

_____

Baked, fried, mashed or in gravy, French fries come from me, straight or wavy.

_____

262. Circle the items you can eat.

263. Place the vehicles in the correct group.

Bicycle   Car   Rocket   Helicopter
Submarine   Boat   Airplane
Truck   Ship

Land	Air	Water

264. Complete the image using the grid and color it.

265. Match the shapes with the number of sides they have.

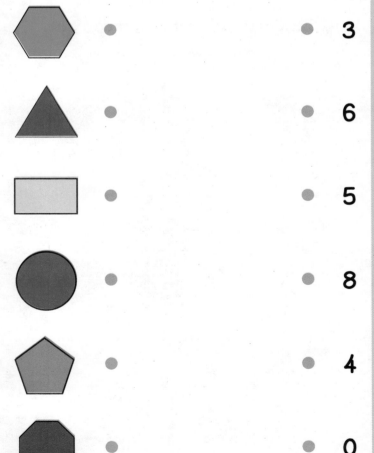

3

6

5

8

4

0

266. Tick the correct top view of the given images.

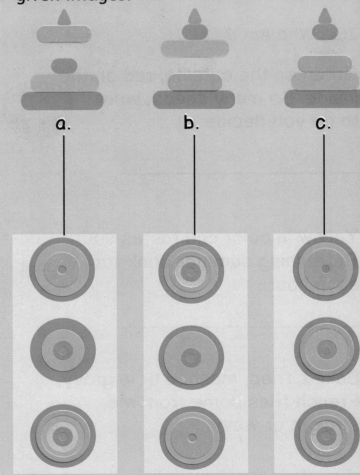

a.   b.   c.

66

267. Match the job and its practitioner.

Singer •   •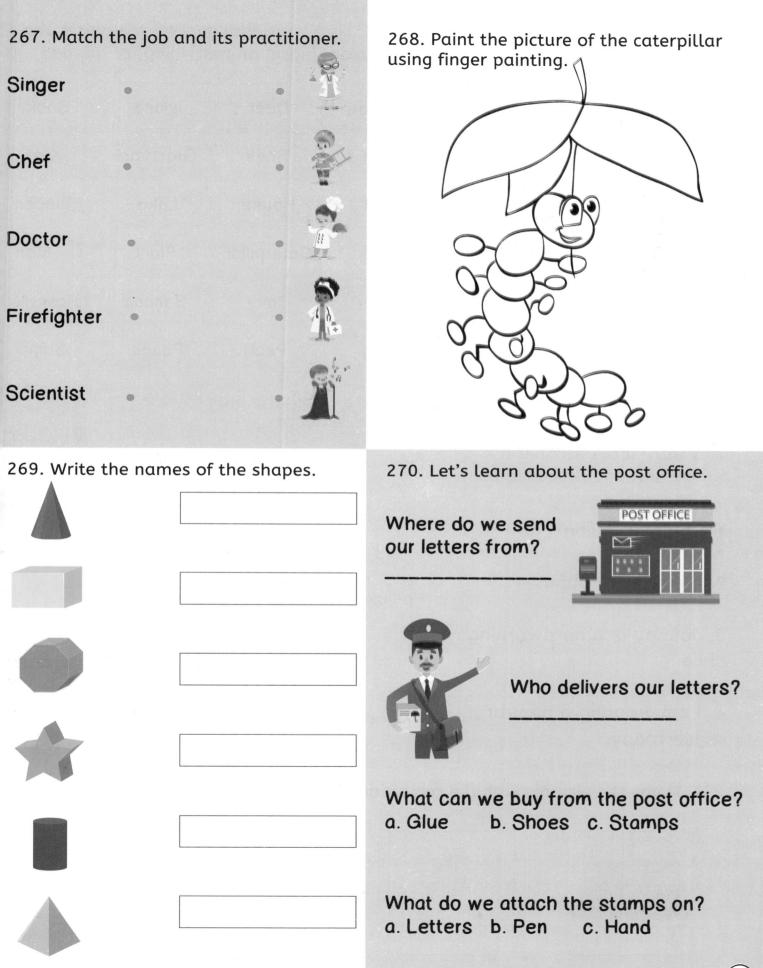

Chef •

Doctor •

Firefighter •

Scientist •

268. Paint the picture of the caterpillar using finger painting.

269. Write the names of the shapes.

270. Let's learn about the post office.

Where do we send our letters from?
_____

Who delivers our letters?
_____

What can we buy from the post office?
a. Glue   b. Shoes   c. Stamps

What do we attach the stamps on?
a. Letters   b. Pen   c. Hand

271. Color the grid as per the given instructions.

If the word is a person, color it green.
If the word is a place, color it red.
If the word is a thing, color it orange.
If the word is an animal or a bird, color it blue.

A Noun is a word that denotes the name of a person, place, animal, thing, or an idea.

Sparrow	Deer	Island	Sock
Pen	Shelf	Grandma	Kid
Girl	House	Lake	Saucer
Desk	Caterpillar	Plant	Man
River	Cave	Banana	Policewoman
Dog	Pearl	Panda	Ship

272. Circle the adjectives in each sentence.

Any word that describes the quality of a noun is called an Adjective.

1. Shelly is a short girl.

2. I like fluffy puppies.

3. Johnny is a hardworking child.

4. I am wearing a beautiful dress today.

273. Circle verbs with blue color in the given sentences.

They ran all the way home.

 I lit the candles.

He bakes the cake in an oven.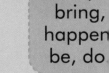

 I am selling books.

I lost my eraser.

Verb

A word a group of words th is used t indicate that somethin happen or exists For example bring, happen be, do

274. Name the pictures with the correct double letter words.

275. Write the plural forms of the following words.

Frame _____

Bench _____

Tree _____

Brush _____

276. Look at the pictures and circle the right answers.

Kaira is putting on her favorite -
Hairbands, Hairband

The rainbow has seven -
Color, Colors

She combs her -
Hairs, Hair

277. Write the opposites of the following words.

Clean _____

Difficult _____

Right _____

Soft _____

Enemy _____

278. Fill in the blanks with the correct prepositions from the box.

on
in
near
between
under

1. The bag is _____ the table.

2. The bird is _____ the sheet.

3. The cat is _____ the bed.

4. The gift is _____ the bed and dog.

5. The table is _____ the room.

279. Match the contractions correctly with the words.

Are not •   • We'd

We would •   • They've

There is •   • Aren't

They have •   • There's

Who is •   • He'd

He had •   • Who's

280. Circle the noun.

My sister enjoys watching television.

281. Color the number of glasses that can be filled with the juice in  = 100ml
the jug.

| 400ml | | | | | |
| 500ml | | | | | |

282. Arrange the given numbers in ascending order.

| 327 | 382 |
| 361 | 312 |

| 618 | 655 |
| 624 | 611 |

283. Solve and write answers in the boxes.

6x5

9-2

4+4

8÷2

70

284. Answer the following questions with reference to the clock.

a. What is the time on the clock?

_ _ _ _ _ _ _ _ _ _ _ _ _ _ _ _ _

b. How many hours are there in one day?

_ _ _ _ _ _ _ _ _ _ _ _ _ _ _ _ _

c. What is the half of 12 hours?

_ _ _ _ _ _ _ _ _ _ _ _ _ _ _ _ _

285. If the burger is 150g and the apple is 15g, how many apples will be equal to the weight of 1 burger?

286. Look at the teapot and write the number on the label.

6 tens + 4 ones =

4 tens + 8 ones =

5 tens + 1 ones =

3 tens + 8 ones =

3 tens + 2 ones =

287. Use the value given to each monster to solve the sums.

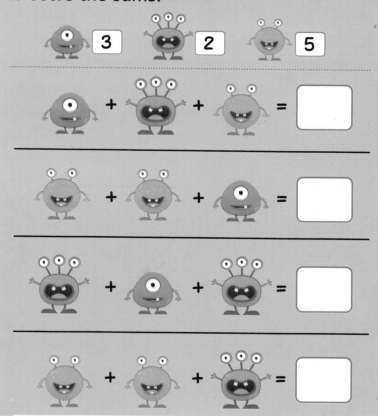

288. Color according to the given fractions.

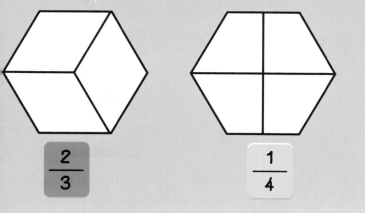

$\dfrac{2}{3}$

$\dfrac{1}{4}$

289. Subtract the numbers on top and write the answers in the bubble below.

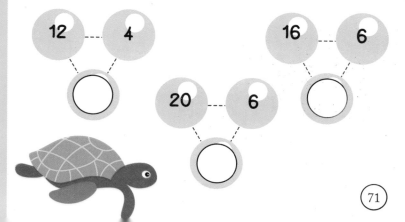

12 --- 4

16 --- 6

20 --- 6

290. Are these living (L) or non-living (NL) things?

( )	( )	( )

( )	( )	( )

291. Mrs. Jones wants to bake a cake. Help her find the ingredients at the supermarket.

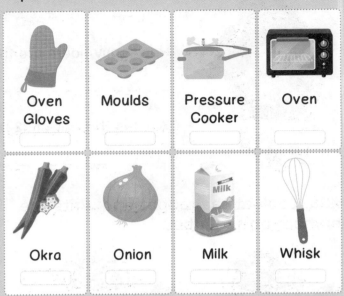

Oven Gloves	Moulds	Pressure Cooker	Oven
Okra	Onion	Milk	Whisk

292. Name a vegetable that is green in color.

_____

293. Name a vegetable that has many layers.

_____

294. Name a vegetable that is red in color.

_____

295. Name a vegetable that you can eat raw

_____

296. Veg or non veg? Write in the blank spaces provided.

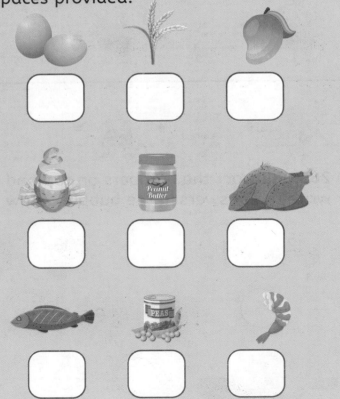

297. Circle the activities that are done fo a longer time.

1. Doing Homework / Putting on Shoes

2. Brushing Teeth / Eating Breakfast

3. Washing Hands / Writing an Essay

72

298. What color will you get after the experiment?

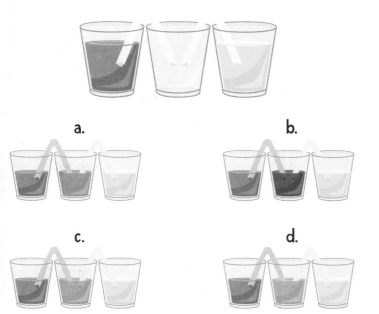

a.

b.

c.

d.

299. What grows in the garden?

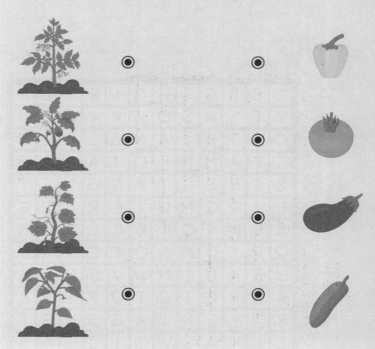

300. Match and sort out the waste.

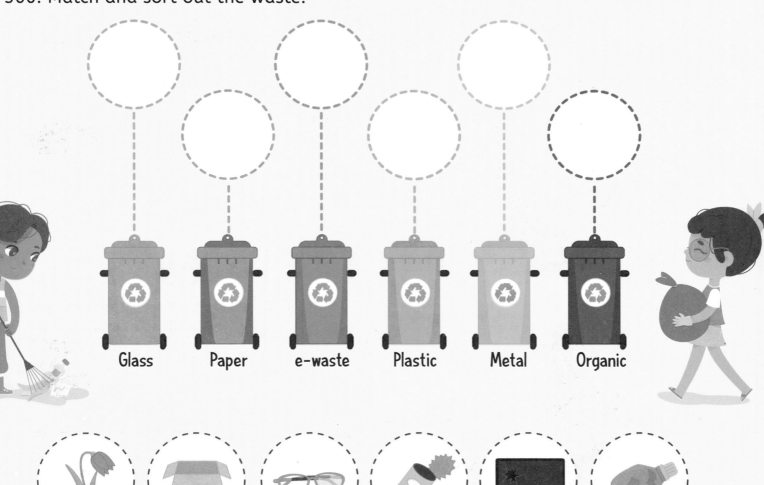

Glass Paper e-waste Plastic Metal Organic

a. b. c. d. e. f.

301. Find the given shapes in the word search box.

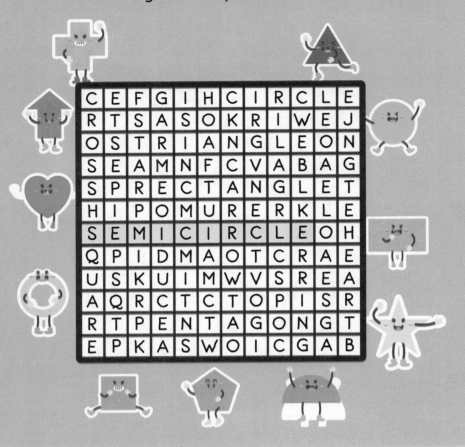

C	E	F	G	I	H	C	I	R	C	L	E
R	T	S	A	S	O	K	R	I	W	E	J
O	S	T	R	I	A	N	G	L	E	O	N
S	E	A	M	N	F	C	V	A	B	A	G
S	P	R	E	C	T	A	N	G	L	E	T
H	I	P	O	M	U	R	E	R	K	L	E
S	E	M	I	C	I	R	C	L	E	O	H
Q	P	I	D	M	A	O	T	C	R	A	E
U	S	K	U	I	M	W	V	S	R	E	A
A	Q	R	C	T	C	T	O	P	I	S	R
R	T	P	E	N	T	A	G	O	N	G	T
E	P	K	A	S	W	O	I	C	G	A	B

303. Color the bear on bike.

302. Circle the things unrelated to the sensory organs.

304. Circle the face you would make in these situations.

306. Your parents got you a puppy as your birthday gift. Draw the emoticon to express your feeling.

305. Match the animals with their homes.

307. Connect the dots from 1 to 15.

308. Match the vegetables on the left with their halves on the right.

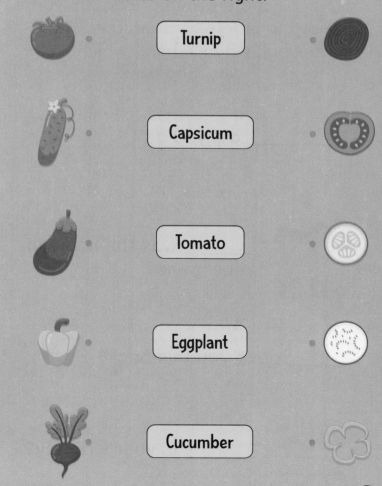

Turnip

Capsicum

Tomato

Eggplant

Cucumber

309. Fill in the blanks using the given words.

| Firefighter | Teacher | Author | Pilot |

She teaches in a school. She is a
_____ .

He flies the airplane. He is a
_____ .

She puts out the fire. She is a
_____ .

He writes books. He is an
_____.

310. Look at the images and complete the sentences.

1. The man is picking
_____ from the garden.

2. I like drinking _____
in the morning.

3. The _____ walks
very slowly.

311. Fill in the blanks using the 'WH' words.

WH words are a group of English words used to introduce questions. These are what, when, where, which, who, why, and how.

_____ did you go?

_____ was the name of
your friend?

_____ gave you this book?

_____ is your birthday?

312. Find the given words in the word search box.

E	K	Q	V	N	B	H	Q	P
S	C	L	E	A	N	C	M	L
L	F	S	H	M	N	U	C	A
E	Z	C	E	C	I	Q	P	Y
E	H	E	A	R	T	E	A	X
P	D	F	L	D	P	N	B	G
F	I	T	T	N	I	O	K	W
D	K	T	H	E	W	L	F	P

Fit Health Play Sleep

Heart Clean

313. Read and answer the following questions.

> Hi. My name is Sara. A week ago, my dad brought me a new pet. It is a cute little puppy. It is two months old. I call it Dodo.
> Dodo loves to sleep as much as he loves to play. My mom and dad help me tend to Dodo and keep him clean. My mom helped me make a kennel for him. Every day after school, I take Dodo for a walk. I love Dodo.

1. When did Sara's dad bring her a new pet?

_____

2. What did Sara name her puppy?

_____

3. What does her new pet love to do?

_____

314. Find the rhyming words from each row.

Rode	Table	Cent	Cable
Game	Name	Blurred	Write
Threw	Giant	Throw	Low
Leak	Late	Speak	Loop
Run	Tons	Lot	Bun
Call	Cell	Shell	Curl

315. Write 3 adjectives to describe yourself.

_____

_____

_____

316. Write 3 adjectives to describe your best friend.

_____

_____

_____

317. Study the graph and answer the questions that follow.

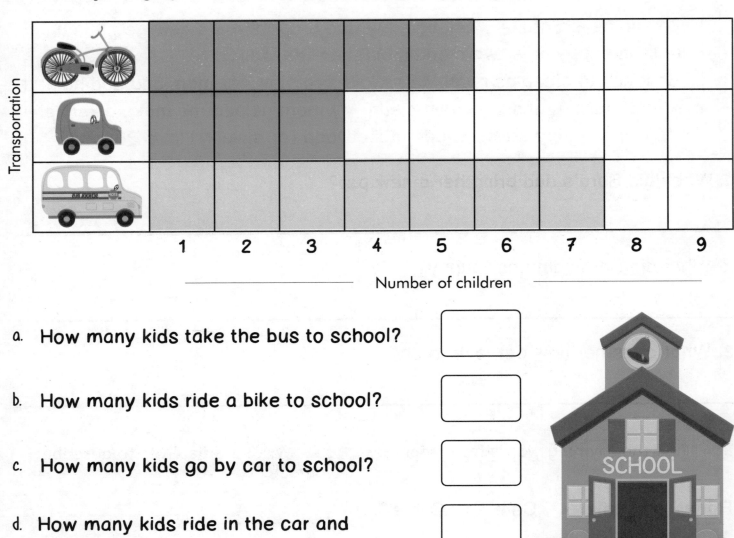

Transportation

Number of children

a. How many kids take the bus to school?

b. How many kids ride a bike to school?

c. How many kids go by car to school?

d. How many kids ride in the car and bus in total?

318. Tally the sea animals and answer the question accordingly.

Which animal has the highest count and by how much?

_ _

319. Show your mealtimes on the clocks. Write time in the blank space.

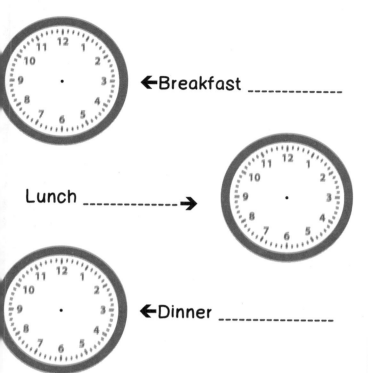

←Breakfast _____

Lunch _ _ _ _ _ _ _ _ _ _→

←Dinner _____

320. Write the answers in numbers.

	seconds in one minute
	minutes in one hour
	hours in one day
	days in one week
	weeks in one year
	months in one year
	days in one year
	seasons in one year

321. Match the numbers on the clock.

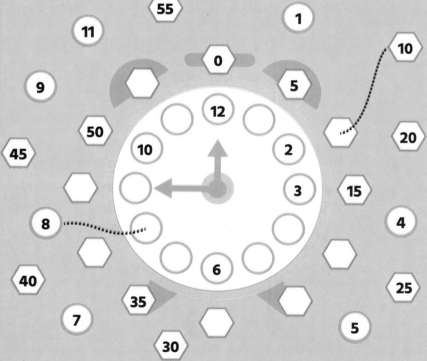

323. Tick the correct time.

a.
- ◯ 6 o'clock
- ◯ 8 o'clock
- ◯ 4 o'clock

b.
- ◯ 1 o'clock
- ◯ 3 o'clock
- ◯ 5 o'clock

325. Read both the hands in the clock and write the time in both ways.

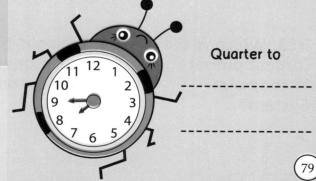

Quarter to

_ _ _ _ _ _ _ _ _ _ _

_ _ _ _ _ _ _ _ _ _ _

324. My swimming class starts at 4 pm and ends at 6 pm. What is the duration of the class?

326. Identify the flags and write the names of the countries.

 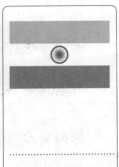    

327. Match the countries with their capital cities.

France   Italy   Egypt   India
•   •   •   •

•   •   •   •
New   Cairo   Rome   Paris
Delhi

328. Answer the following questions.

Name the coldest continent.

....

Name the hottest continent.

....

Name the smallest continent.

....

329. Which is the closest planet to the Sun?

330. Which planet is farthest from the Sun?

331. Which planet has a prominent ring around it?

332. The Earth completes one rotation in how many hours?

333. Which is the largest planet in the Solar System?

334. Which is the smallest planet in the Solar System?

335. The fixed path in which planets revolve is called?

336. The Earth completes one revolution in how many days?

337. Label the pictures using the words given below.

Eruption, Hurricane, Tornado, Earthquake

------------------   ------------------

------------------   ------------------

338. Circle how the following things feel.

cold / hot

soft / thorny

greasy / dry

339. Which clothes are worn in winter? Tick the circle.

○   ○   ○   ○   ○

341. I am a baby lion. I am called a
   a. cub   b. calf   c. puppy

_____

340. Match the animals and their homes.

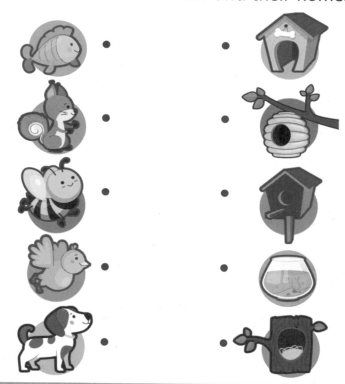

342. Put (✓) on countable things (✗) on uncountable things.

sugar   apples   leaves   water   books   rice

☐   ☐   ☐   ☐   ☐   ☐

343. Multiply the row and column to complete the tables.

1	2	3	4	5	6	7	8	9	10
2		6							
3					18				
4									40
5			20						
6						42			
7								63	
8	16								
9				45					
10							80		

344. Solve the multiplications.

a.  X = $3 \times 2 = 6$

b.  X =

c.  X =

345. Multiply the numbers to get the answers.

5 X 7 =

9 X 3 =

4 X 8 =

346. Help the baby animals reach their food through maze by solving the divisions.

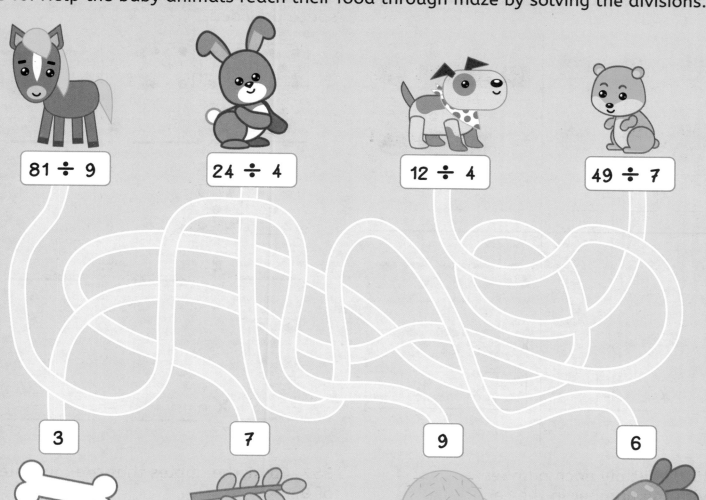

81 ÷ 9   24 ÷ 4   12 ÷ 4   49 ÷ 7

3   7   9   6

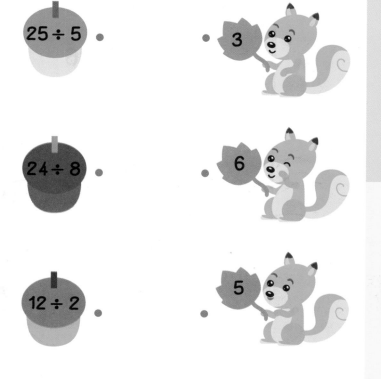

347. Match the following.

25 ÷ 5 •   • 3

24 ÷ 8 •   • 6

12 ÷ 2 •   • 5

348. Solve the division problems.

42 ÷ 2 = ☐   88 ÷ 4 = ☐

69 ÷ 3 = ☐   72 ÷ 6 = ☐

65 ÷ 5 = ☐   32 ÷ 8 = ☐

349. 80 people have been invited to a banquet. The caterer is arranging tables. Each table can seat 10 people. How many tables are needed?

350. Count and multiply the given images.

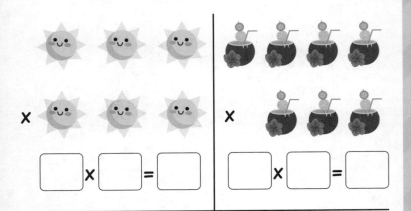

[ ] × [ ] = [ ]   [ ] × [ ] = [ ]

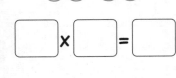
[ ] × [ ] = [ ]

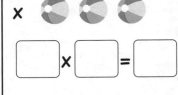
[ ] × [ ] = [ ]

351. Solve and write the answers in the space provided.

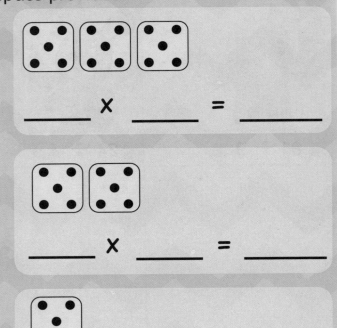

_____ × _____ = _____

_____ × _____ = _____

_____ × _____ = _____

352. Multiply each number with the number in the center to complete the web.

353. Color the apples that are multiples of 9.

4   16

9   36

354. Solve the following multiplications and have a fun day.

3 X 10

6 X 10

5 X 10

8 X 10

355. Identify the mathematical symbols and match them with their names.

 •
 •
 •
 •
 •
 •
 •
 •

• Equal to

• Less than

• Addition

• Subtraction

• Percent

• Greater than

• Division

• Multiplication

356. Help Tina solve the following two-digit divisions.

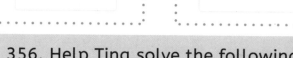

75 ÷ 5 =

35 ÷ 7 =

81 ÷ 9 =

39 ÷ 3 =

357. Select three pumpkins whose numbers add to give the sum equal to 30.

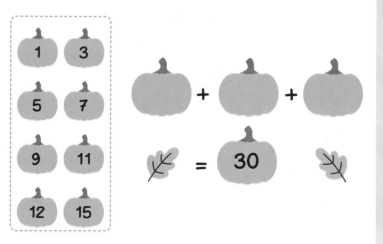

1 3
5 7
9 11
12 15

+ +

= 30

358. Write the numbers using the place values.

1 thousands + 4 hundreds + 7 tens + 1 ones =

6 thousands + 2 hundreds + 4 tens + 9 ones =

3 thousands + 1 hundreds + 0 tens + 2 ones =

359. Fill in the boxes with the correct letters to get the names of the objects.

T=1 A=3 B=2 O=4

2   4   3   1

C=1 L=3 I=5 P=2 E=4 N=6

2   4   6   1   5   3

360. Write eight hundred and fifty-four in numbers.

_____

361. Subtract 9 from 20.

_____

362. Complete the pattern:

3, 6, 9 ___ , ___ 18, 21, ___ , ___ , 30

363. What comes after 101?

_____

364. Read carefully and fill in the blanks.

• 4 x 5 = 20, then 20 ÷ 4 = _____

• 7 x 3 = 21, then 21 ÷ 7 = _____

• 9 x 4 = 36, then 36 ÷ 9 = _____

• 4 x 8 = 32, then 32 ÷ 4 = _____

• 1 x 6 = 6, then 6 ÷ 1 = _____

• 5 x 5 = 25, then 25 ÷ 5 = _____

365. Help Matt solve the following two-digit divisions.

 81 ÷ 3 =

 49 ÷ 7 =

 99 ÷ 9 =

366. It's raining numbers. Arrange them in ascending order in the box given below.

65   100   98   28   17   35   54

99   8   1   9   67   87

367. Color the dices to get the sum equal to the given numbers.

    7

    12

   9

    4

368. Answer the questions by choosing the correct number.

| 1000 639 700 220 485 |

Number between 950 and 1050.

Number between 600 and 650.

Number you get if you multiply 7 by 100.

Number smaller than 300.

Number bigger than 400 but smaller than 490.

369. Use >, < or = correctly.

62		39	29		29
72		44	38		76
43		90	12		21
22		10	18		19
9		19	5		5
88		99	89		98

370. Solve the circular addition.

5	+	....	=	12
+		+		+
8	+	3	=	....
=		=		=
....	+	10	=	23

371. Arrange the hats in descending order.

----

372. Arrange the hats in ascending order.

----

373. Color the fish with the greater number.

a.
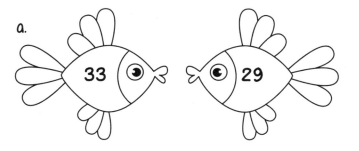
33   29

b.
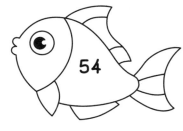
45   54

374. I have two wheels and a bell in front,
Ride me to stay fit or perform stunt.
What am I?

375. Rectangular in shape with six wheels,
I carry students to school in all zeals.
What am I?

376. I am not a bird in the sky,
But I have wings and I fly.
What am I?

377. Petrol or diesel or long ride,
Four wheels on road, "roll tide"!
What am I?

378. Practice your writing skills.

1. I am good at _____
_____.

2. I am bad at _____
_____.

3. I don't like _____
because _____.

4. I like _____
because _____.

5. I love to play _____
_____.

6. I don't like to play _____
_____.

7. My favorite movie is _____
because _____.

379. Match the idioms to their meanings.

A dark horse •   • Unable to see well

A copycat •   • Someone who isn't favored in a group

To smell a rat •   • To be pleasant and caring

As blind as a bat •   • A surprise competitor

A black sheep •   • Someone who copies others

As gentle as a lamb •   • To detect something suspicious

380. Replace the underlined words with their antonyms and write the word.

1. It was a cold day. _____

2. My father braids my curly hair every morning. _____

3. He got the answer right. _____

4. Cathy's game is better than Carl's game. _____

5. Can you please place the warm bowl on the table? _____

6. The strawberry tasted incredibly sweet. _____

381. Fill in the blanks with suitable pronouns.

1. Ronit is buying a gift for his friends. _____ is going to give _____ a flower vase.

2. Please don't trouble that dog. _____ may bite _____.

382. Complete the sentences using the correct option.

I will _____ you at the game. (meet, meat)

What did you _____ from the supermarket? (buy, bye)

383. Family time! How much do you know your family?

	MOTHER	FATHER	SIBLINGS
Name			
Occupation			
Favorite Food			
Favorite Color			
Hobbies			

384. Do you like outdoor games or indoor activities?

I like ....

because ....

....

....

....

....

....

385. What is your favorite subject in school?

386. Draw and paint your favorite flower.

387. Rearrange the letters to get a cute little animal. SILRQUER

388. Which game has royal pieces in it?

389. Draw and color your favorite emoticon.

390. Which is your favorite ice cream?

391. Draw and paint the fruit you like the most.

392. Name your favorite wild animal.

393. Where do you like to spend your free time?

394. Draw and color a Rubik's cube.

395. Do you like ice cream in a cone or in a cup?

396. Decorate an egg with your own design.

397. Design a Halloween pumpkin.

398. Which is your favorite pet animal?

399. Draw a bird.

400. Draw an autumn leaf and color it.

401. Color the flags with the right colors.

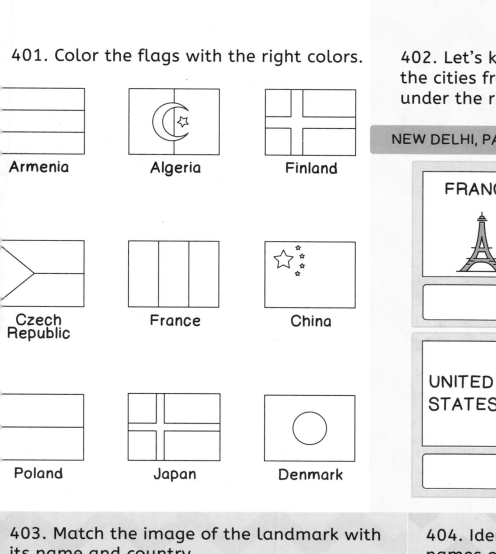

Armenia   Algeria   Finland

Czech Republic   France   China

Poland   Japan   Denmark

402. Let's know world capitals! Pick the cities from the box and place them under the right country.

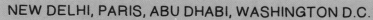

NEW DELHI, PARIS, ABU DHABI, WASHINGTON D.C.

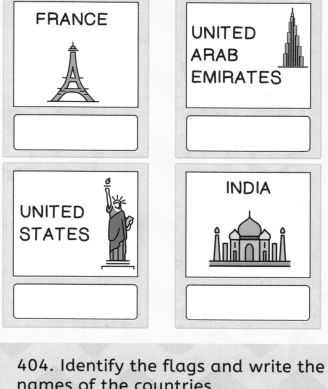

FRANCE

UNITED ARAB EMIRATES

UNITED STATES

INDIA

403. Match the image of the landmark with its name and country.

- Stonehenge, England
- Colosseum, Italy
- Eiffel Tower, France
- Sphinx, Egypt
- White House, USA

404. Identify the flags and write the names of the countries.

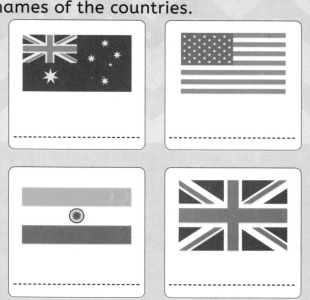

--------------------- ---------------------

--------------------- ---------------------

405. Design your own flag and color it with your favorite colors.

406. Fill in the numbers such that the sum of each side is equal to the other.

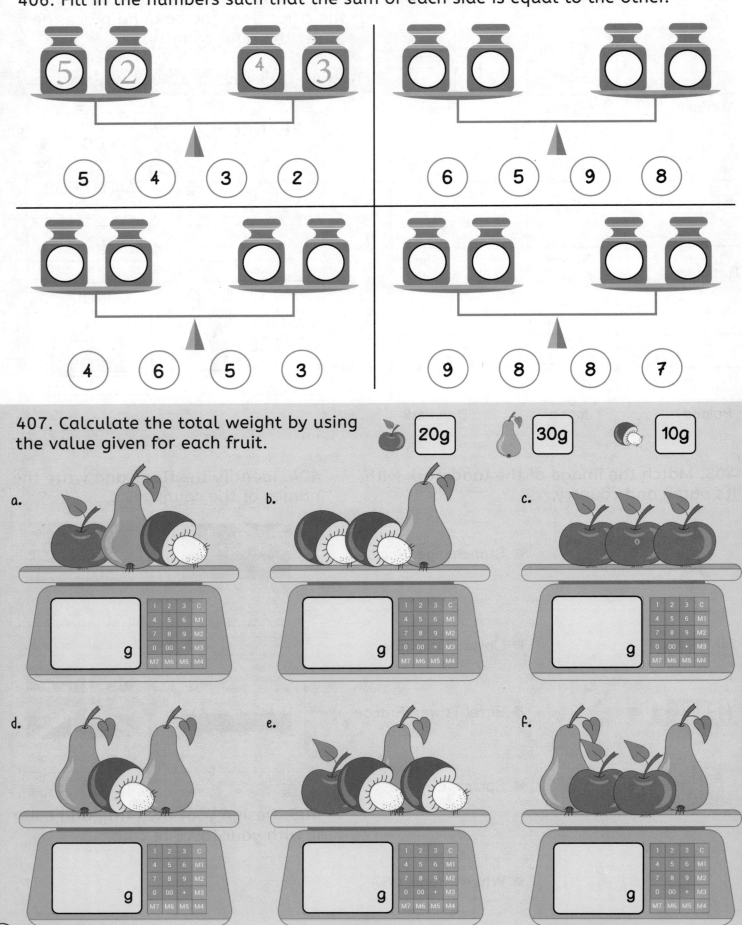

407. Calculate the total weight by using the value given for each fruit.

apple 20g   pear 30g   kiwi 10g

a.

b.

c.

d.

e.

f.

408. Write the total by adding the value given to each object.

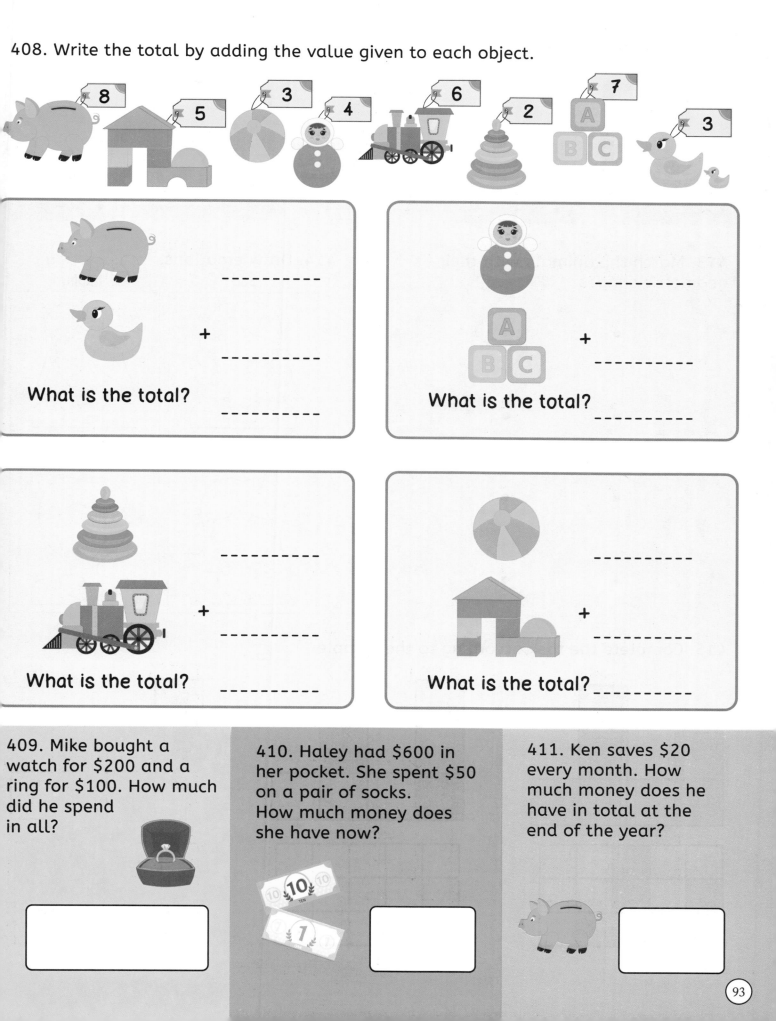

8   5   3   4   6   2   7   3

What is the total?

_____
\+
_____

_____

What is the total?

_____
\+
_____

_____

What is the total?

_____
\+
_____

What is the total? _____
\+
_____

409. Mike bought a watch for $200 and a ring for $100. How much did he spend in all?

410. Haley had $600 in her pocket. She spent $50 on a pair of socks. How much money does she have now?

411. Ken saves $20 every month. How much money does he have in total at the end of the year?

412. Match the emotions and face.

413. Match the animals with their geometric shapes.

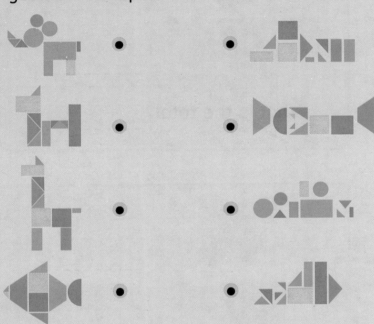 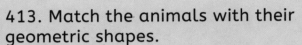    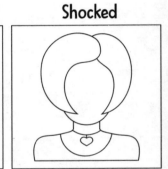

414. Draw emotions.

Sad	Happy

Surprised	Shocked

415. Complete the task according to the sample.

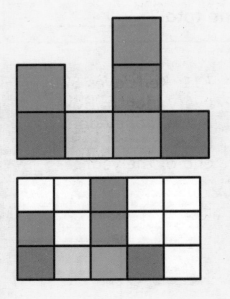 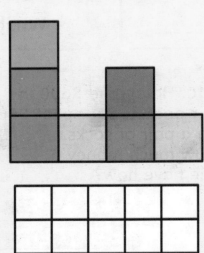 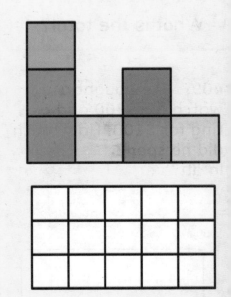

416. Find the hidden objects.

417. What do these animals say?

418. What begins with T, finishes with T, and has T in it?

419. You cut me, slice me, dice me, and all the while, you cry. What am I?

420. What do you call a cat who loves to swim?

421. Observe the picture and color the shapes in it accordingly.

422. Draw lines to match the opposites.

in

hot

short

cold

long

out

423. Count and write the number of fruits in the boxes given below.

424. Circle the option on the right that matches with the vehicle on the left.

425. Circle the correct trash can for the waste on the left.

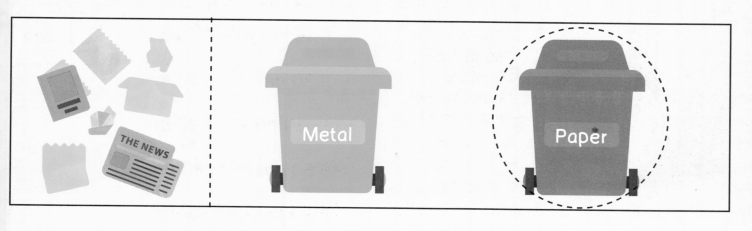

426. Answer the following questions.

a. The clock is 30 minutes forward. What is the right time?

b. The clock is 45 minutes behind. What is the correct time?

----

428. Match the time in numbers with words.

4:15 •	• Five past two.
3:30 •	• Quarter past four.
2:05 •	• Nine o'clock.
7:45 •	• Five to five.
4:55 •	• Half past three.
9:00 •	• Quarter to eight.

427. How much time has passed? Think and write.

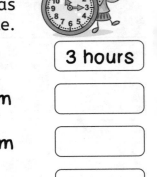

6:15 pm to 9:15 pm	3 hours
8:30 am to 12:00 pm	
12:20 pm. to 1:00 pm	
9:50 am to 11:40 am	
5:00 pm to 5:45 pm	
3:30 pm to 6:30 pm	

429. Fill in the blanks.

_____ seconds = 1 minute

60 minutes = __ hour

__ days = 1 week

12 _____ = 1 year

___ days = 1 year

4 weeks = __ month

430. How many minutes are shown in colored part of the clocks?

a.

b.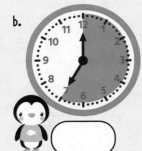

431. Solve and write the missing numbers.

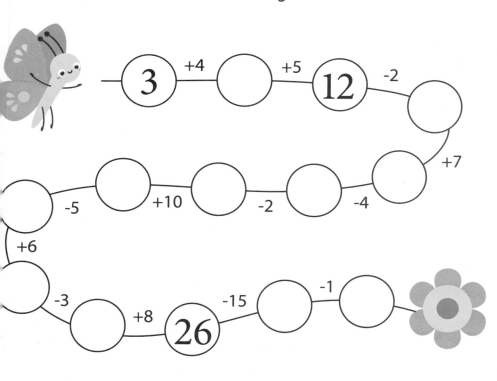

**432. If it's true, color ⬛.
If it's false, color ⬛.**

a. | 3 | = | 3 | ⬜

b. | 5 | < | 4 | ⬜

c. | 6 | < | 8 | ⬜

d. | 1 | > | 4 | ⬜

e. | 9 | = | 7 | ⬜

433. Write the number that comes out of the robot.

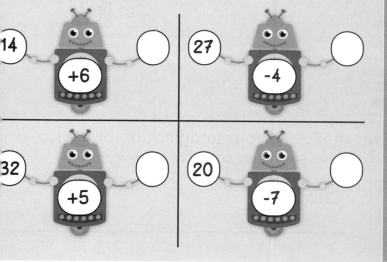

434. Balance the scales.

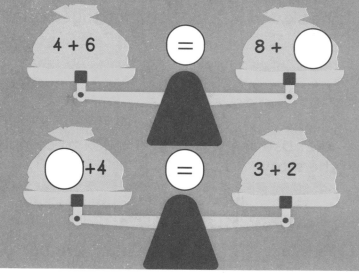

435. Solve the problem train from left to right.

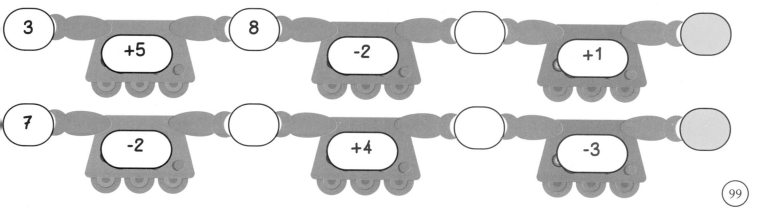

436. Where are they?

Where is the rabbit?
a. On the table
b. Next to the table
c. Under the table

Where is the dog?
a. Behind the box
b. Next to the box
c. Under the box

Where is the cat?
a. Next to the boxes
b. Behind the boxes
c. Between the boxes

437. Fill in the correct question words in the following sentences.

_____ is your hobby?

_____ will you return?

_____ is playing with the dog?

_____ do you do in the evening

_____ cat is in the tree?

_____ many fruits are there in the basket?

438. It is the color of the sky.

439. It helps stick things together.

440. You can sit on it.

441. You go here to learn.

442. Use the words in the box to complete the story.

Favorite	Name	Bake
Cakes	Aunt's	Baker

Hi. My _____ is Ahana. I am a

_____. I can _____ all kinds of

cookies, _____, and muffins. My

personal _____ is the chocolate

cake. I work in my _____ bakery.

443. Use your imagination and write a few sentences on the given topic.

Children

_____

_____

_____

_____

_____

_____

444. Put rhyming words in each basket and write them in their columns.

Basket 1: Snake Mouse Bright Narrow Bunch Sink

Basket 1

Basket 2: Pink Sparrow Lunch House Light Bake

Basket 2

....
....
....
....
....

445. Arrange the following words in alphabetical order.

Party	1.
Cub	2.
Astronaut	3.
Horse	4.
Ball	5.
Rose	6.
Nose	7.
King	8.
Gun	9.
Ship	10.

446. Solve the crossword.

447. Complete the sentences with the most suitable adverbs.

Outside Totally Beautifully Quickly Nicely Early

1. She always speaks _____.

2. She _____ gets me.

3. The children love to play

_____.

4. He plays the piano

_____.

5. She arrived _____ for the

meeting.

6. He ate the entire meal

_____.

101

448. Count and write the different things you see in this picture?

449. Can you name the place described in the picture?

450. What is the color of animals and other objects you see in the above picture?

451. Describe the picture that you see.

----

452. Write the missing numbers.

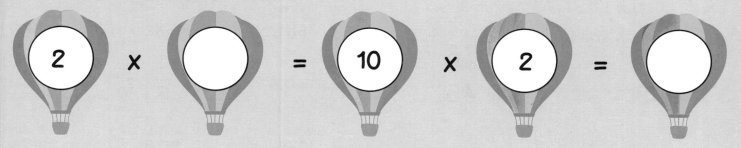

$$2 \times \boxed{} = 10 \qquad 10 \times 2 = \boxed{}$$

453. Match the multiplications with their answers.

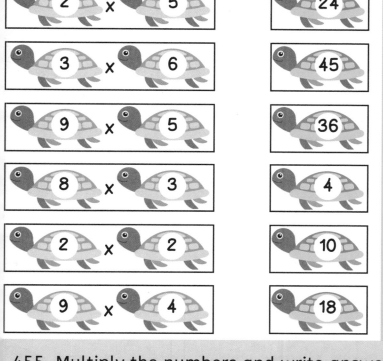

2 × 5 → 24
3 × 6 → 45
9 × 5 → 36
8 × 3 → 4
2 × 2 → 10
9 × 4 → 18

454. Solve the multiplication problems.

$$9 \times 5 = \boxed{}$$

$$11 \times 2 = \boxed{}$$

$$6 \times 6 = \boxed{}$$

$$8 \times 3 = \boxed{}$$

$$4 \times 4 = \boxed{}$$

$$7 \times 8 = \boxed{}$$

455. Multiply the numbers and write answers on each coach.

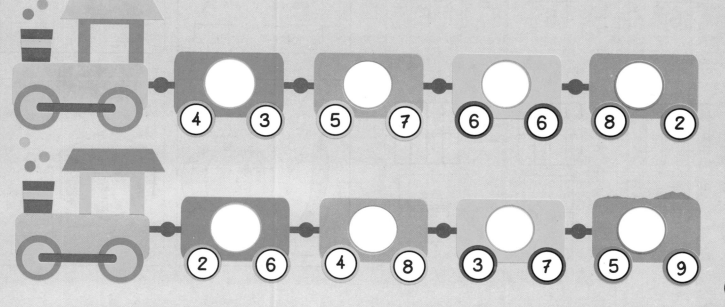

4 3   5 7   6 6   8 2

2 6   4 8   3 7   5 9

456. Solve the following subtractions.

98 − 19	76 − 45

66 − 10	63 − 24

94 − 55	45 − 18

457. Complete the table of 16.

16X1	16X2	16X3
16X4	16X5	16X6
16X7	16X8	
16X9	16X10	

458. Observe the example and solve the fraction that follows.

$$\frac{4}{6} - \frac{3}{6} = \frac{1}{6}$$

459. Look at the picture in each box and tick (✓) the lighter one.

104

460. Fill in the blanks with the correct numbers to get the given sum.

 (....) + (10) + (15) = (30)

 (9) + (....) + (8) = (30)

 (13) + (12) + (....) = (32)

 (8) + (11) + (....) = (25)

 (....) + (3) + (8) = (19)

461. Fun with numbers! Read the numbers and answer the following questions.

| 5 | 4 | 0 | 8 |

Make the smallest and largest four-digit number from the given digits.

....

Make the smallest four-digit number that starts from 5.

....

462. Kacy bought a dress for $20 and a watch for $10. How much did she spend in all?

463. Miles had $60 in her pocket. She spent $50. How much money does she have now?

464. Ken got $40 from his mom, $20 from his dad and $10 from his brother. How much money he has in total?

465. Match the following numbers with their roman numerals.

466. Write the age according to the candles.

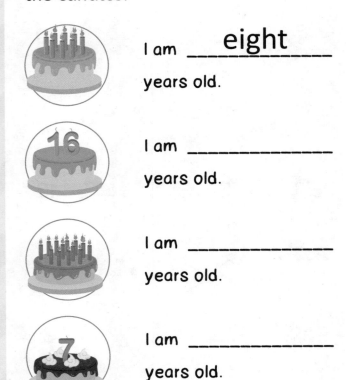

I am ___eight___ years old.

I am _____ years old.

I am _____ years old.

I am _____ years old.

467. Color the first, third, sixth, and seventh flowers.

Color the second, third, fifth, and ninth stars.

Color the fourth, sixth, eighth, and tenth hearts.

Color the first, third, fifth, and seventh flowers.

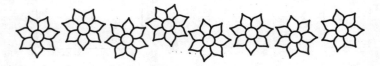

468. Tick 'true' or 'false'.

All living things need food.

True   False

Plants need water to grow.

True   False

The Earth is flat.

True   False

Plants need oxygen.

True   False

The giraffe is the largest animal.

True   False

469. Match the animals with their young ones.

470. Mark the body parts of the bird with the correct number.

1. Beak   2. Body   3. Eye
4. Claw   5. Head   6. Tail
7. Wings

471. Color the animals you have seen in real life.

472. Count the number of squares.

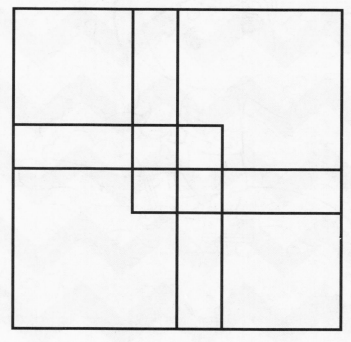

Answer: _____

473. Place the clothes in matching wardrobes by writing the numbers in the boxes.

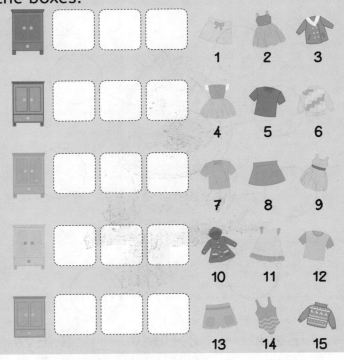

474. Trace and complete the pattern. Color it brightly.

475. Name the things you see and color the image.

476. Pick the odd one out.

477. Where do Eskimos live?

478. What is a house on wheels called?

479. Circle the animal that makes the sound given on the left.

Oink Oink			
Meow			
Neigh			
Moo			
Woof Woof			

480. Each mouse is missing something. Draw the missing part.

481. Observe the picture carefully and answer the questions.

How many rabbits in total?	How many clouds in the sky?	How many flowers on the ground?

482. Help the bear reach the honey pot.

483. Choose the correct month to complete the sentences.

October   January   December   February

_____ has 28 days and in leap year has 29.

Christmas falls in the month of _____.

_____ is the first month of the year.

Autumn falls in the months of September and _____.

484. What comes before?

◯ ···· ◯ ···· **23**

◯ ···· ◯ ···· **27**

◯ ···· ◯ ···· **25**

◯ ···· ◯ ···· **26**

485. Solve the following.

🌷=5   🌷=3   🌷=4   🌷=2

🌷🌷🌷 - 🌷🌷 = ☐

🌷🌷🌷 - 🌷🌷🌷 = ☐

🌷🌷 - 🌷 = ☐

🌷🌷🌷 - 🌷🌷 = ☐

486. Draw the hands on the clock to tell the end time.

Start Time   End Time

4:00

The game is **3** hours long.

487. Amy went to the park with Mary at 4:00. They played for 3 hours. At what time did they finish playing?

....

488. Jake finished watching his favorite show. The show was 2 hours long and now it's 7:00. At what time did the show start?

....

489. Can you write the fractions? The first one has been done for you.

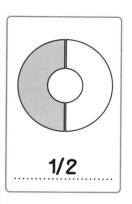
1/2

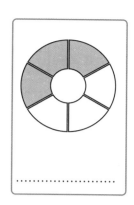
....

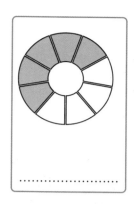
....

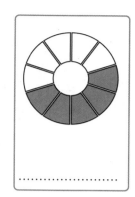
....

....

490. Choose the correct fraction.

$\frac{1}{3}$	$\frac{2}{3}$

$\frac{6}{2}$	$\frac{4}{5}$

$\frac{4}{7}$	$\frac{5}{8}$

$\frac{4}{6}$	$\frac{9}{3}$

491. Match the images and the fractions.

$\frac{3}{7}$ $\frac{3}{5}$

$\frac{2}{7}$ $\frac{4}{7}$ $\frac{1}{8}$

$\frac{2}{5}$

$\frac{1}{5}$ $\frac{6}{9}$ $\frac{5}{6}$

492. Choose the correct fraction.

$\frac{2}{6}$	$\frac{5}{6}$	$\frac{3}{6}$

$\frac{4}{7}$	$\frac{2}{7}$	$\frac{1}{7}$

$\frac{1}{4}$	$\frac{2}{4}$

$\frac{3}{4}$

493. Spot five differences between the two bouquets.

494. Complete the pattern.

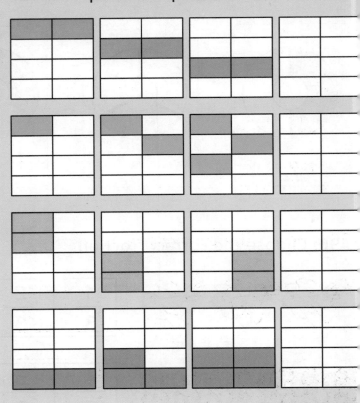

495. Match the shapes and their names.

cylinder

cube

cuboid

sphere

cone

pyramid

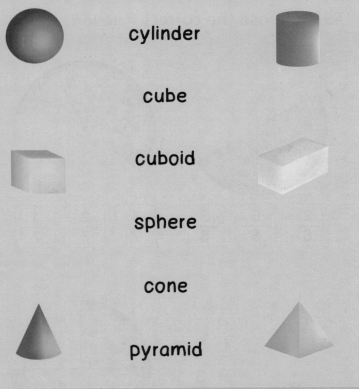

496. Trace the lines to reach the hot-air balloons.

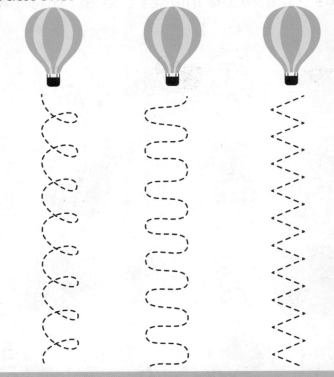

497. Look around and name 5 round things that you can see.

498. Complete the pattern.

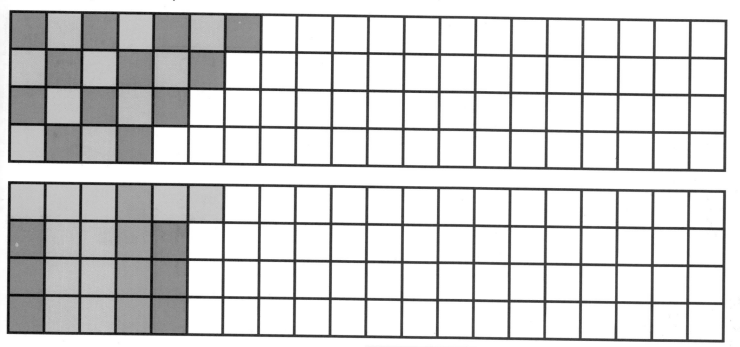

499. Join the dots, name the animal and color it.

500. Help the little girl find her way to the mango tree.

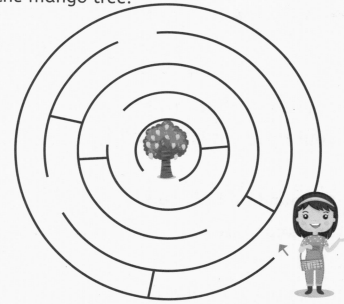

501. Write the names of the birds.

502. Read the clues to find the double letter words that are hidden in the word search box. Write the double letter word in the space next to each clue.

C	U	F	F	S	G	N	I	G	G	I	D
I	I	J	A	Y	P	D	U	C	L	I	N
T	U	D	H	T	U	L	I	P	E	O	O
E	T	V	S	H	E	L	L	E	B	W	I
S	L	I	V	B	I	A	R	S	N	Q	S
E	U	H	E	U	E	T	A	S	S	D	M
V	N	C	N	O	O	N	S	K	S	Y	U
D	G	L	A	S	S	E	S	S	A	N	F
A	H	A	Z	K	U	M	L	S	R	A	F
I	Q	Z	P	L	A	E	A	A	G	S	I
D	A	Y	C	S	J	N	B	L	P	T	N
J	U	W	O	O	L	T	A	M	L	Y	C

1. You wear these when your eyesight is weak ....

2. Found on beaches and seashores ....

3. Antonym of short ....

4. A plant grows to become this ....

5. End part of a sleeve that has buttons over it ....

6. 12 o'clock in a day ....

7. All cows eat this ....

8. A kind of music genre originated in the US ....

9. Sweaters are knitted of this material ....

10. A cupcake is also called ....

503. Number the words in each row in alphabetical order.

MOON	LION	REST	KITE	AFTER

ZEBRA	SPIDER	QUEUE	HIDE	FOG

504. Match the collective nouns with the correct picture.

A collection of •

A bouquet of •

A bowl of •

A loaf of •

A chest of •

A slice of •

505. Write few lines about your time in the park.

_____

_____

_____

_____

_____

_____

506. Write the plurals of the following words.

PERSON ....

MOUSE ....

STEM ....

OX ....

507. Unscramble the sentence and write it correctly.

in / always / visit / Manali / We / winters.

_____

_____

508. Fill in the blanks with suitable words from the box.

Suzy is a _____ child. She loves to dance and _____. Every day

after school, she practices dance in her _____. She lifts her _____

and points her _____ just like a ballerina. She practices until her

father calls her for _____. After dinner, little Suzy goes to _____.

509. Read the following passage and rearrange the jumbled sentences given below.

Once upon a time there was a mother dog and her little puppy. They lived happily on a farm. The puppy was black with white spots. He was very playful. One day, he walked on the road and almost got hit by a car. 'Don't walk in the road again until you grow up and learn how to cross a street,' said Mamma Dog. 'A long time ago, when I was just a little puppy, I got hit by a car. Luckily, it didn't hurt me too bad. I learned how to cross the road safely then on. I look both ways and I cross only if I don't see or hear a car coming,' added Mamma Dog. 'Yes, Mom, I learned a good lesson today,' answered the little puppy.

1. a / got / by / car / I / hit

_____

2. The / spots / with / puppy / was / white / black

_____

3. Don't / the / in / walk / road

_____

4. lesson / today / I / a / good / learned

_____

510. Find the names of wildlife you spot.

L	H	X	C	V	N	X	T	H	P
I	S	G	I	R	A	F	F	E	A
O	W	A	N	L	X	N	M	O	R
N	I	B	W	U	D	I	N	O	R
X	R	A	U	X	G	I	U	Y	O
Z	K	E	T	T	H	A	O	B	T
T	I	G	E	R	O	L	T	U	Z
M	A	O	K	N	Q	S	G	M	A
E	O	O	W	M	O	N	K	E	Y
O	G	G	E	V	Y	C	V	Q	A

Monkey   Giraffe   Tiger   Rhino
Lion   Emu   Parrot

511. Pick the nouns from the box and place them in the correct category.

Teacher Toothpaste Carpet Ladybug
Mother Catfish Hospital School Police
Nurse Theater Station Barber Cow
Dog Pen Book

PERSON	PLACE	THING	ANIMAL

512. Fill in appropriate words to complete the sentences.

Oceans Marine Water
Cold-blooded Rivers Reptiles

Fishes are _____ animals. They can be found in

_____ or _____. Fish need _____ to

live. These animals are just like _____. They are also

_____ .

513. Color the clouds that are feminine.

Madam   King   Lioness   Tiger

Prince

Siri   Doe   Policewoman

514. Fill in the blanks with the missing letters.

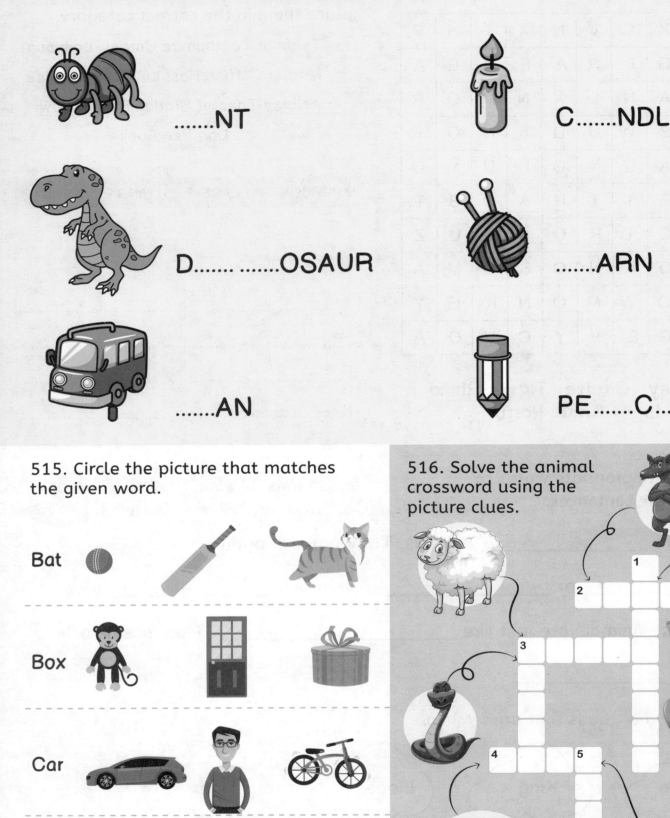

.......NT

C.......NDL.......

D.......... OSAUR

.......ARN

.......AN

PE.......C.......L

515. Circle the picture that matches the given word.

Bat

Box

Car

Ant

516. Solve the animal crossword using the picture clues.

517. Number the flowers from shortest to tallest.

518. Maze fun!

519. Can you spot the 10 differences?

520. Even though I rhyme with beach, you do not find me there. What fruit am I?

521. My name has apple in it, but I neither look nor taste like one. What fruit am I?

522. I am yellow and I grow on trees.
I am popular among monkeys. What fruit am I?

523. I am the king of fruits. I visit you during your summer vacation. What fruit am I?

524. Write the expanded form of the numbers along with their number names and place values.

986 I am expanding.

My number name is

_____

I have

_____ hundreds _____ tens _____ones

_____

My expanded form is

_____ + _____ + _____

116 I am expanding.

My number name is

_____

I have

_____ hundreds _____ tens _____ones

_____

My expanded form is

_____ + _____ + _____

208 I am expanding.

My number name is

_____

I have

_____ hundreds _____ tens _____ones

_____

My expanded form is

_____ + _____ + _____

525. Write the place value of the underlined digits.

3̲49 _____

61̲4 _____

4̲90 _____

25̲4 _____

526. Color the clouds with even numbers.

162   54   12   30

61   10   11   35

69   32   17   12

142   139   14   19

527. Color the flowers with odd numbers

111   121

18   125   112

113   116

528. Cross the odd one out from each box.

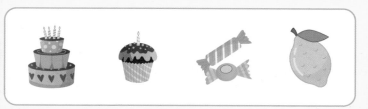

529. Match the seasons to their pictures.

Fall

Summer

Winter

Spring

530. Do you recognize these buildings?

------------------   ------------------   ------------------   ------------------

531. Tick the things that will melt in summer.

Ice cream

Apple

Bread

Ice cube

Chocolate

532. Will these objects sink or float in water? Circle the correct answer.

Sink / Float

Sink / Float

Sink / Float

Sink / Float

Sink / Float

Sink / Float

533. Help the caterpillar reach the leaves.

534. Color the shapes and fill the graph.

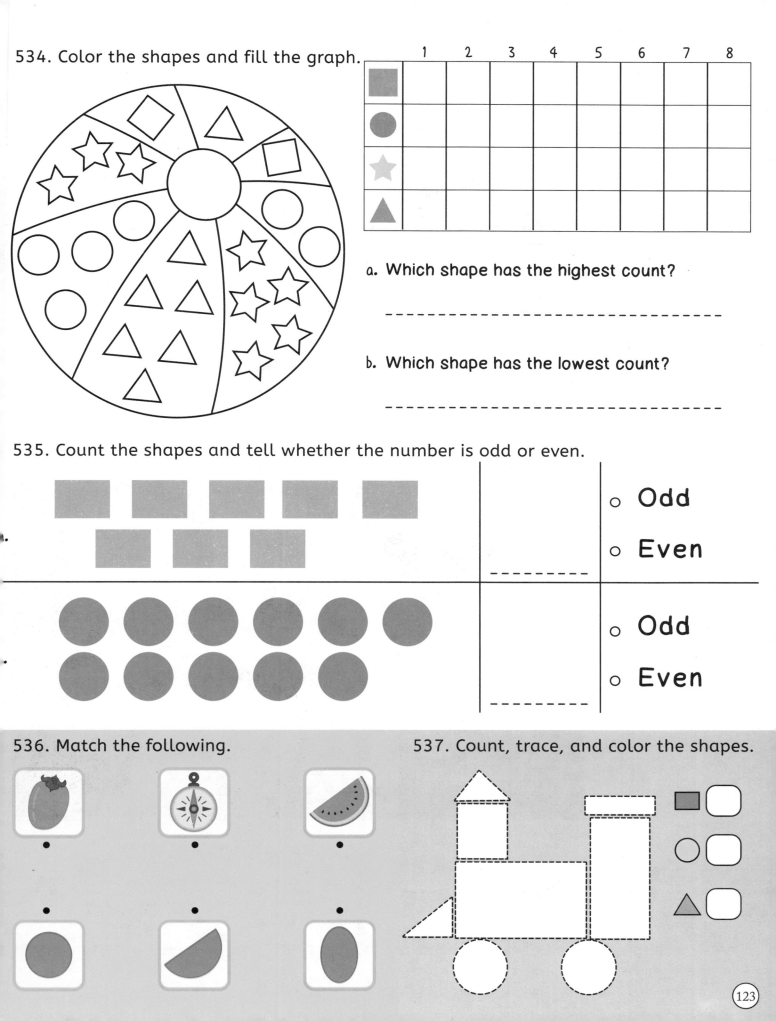

	1	2	3	4	5	6	7	8
■								
●								
★								
▲								

a. Which shape has the highest count?

_____

b. Which shape has the lowest count?

_____

535. Count the shapes and tell whether the number is odd or even.

o **Odd**

o **Even**

_____

o **Odd**

o **Even**

_____

536. Match the following.

537. Count, trace, and color the shapes.

123

538. Find and circle the objects given below.

539. Name the body parts.

540. Who am I?

I help you see.

_____

 I help you eat.

_____

I help you listen.

_____

 I help you smell.

_____

541. Match the sensory organs with the objects associated with it.

542. Word Search.

G	T	A	T	O	R	S	H	J	W
H	K	O	B	X	H	E	A	D	L
M	H	N	E	Z	T	S	L	K	F
E	A	R	T	S	Y	E	B	C	I
W	N	X	L	I	G	H	K	V	N
Q	D	A	F	S	A	C	N	L	G
F	E	R	U	V	H	O	E	A	E
O	J	M	Y	E	A	Y	E	S	R
O	A	G	S	N	G	U	B	V	S
T	S	T	O	M	A	C	H	B	K

Head Ear Fingers Hand

Stomach Knee Foot

543. Match the opposites.

BIG

CLEAN

QUIET

HAPPY

SPRING

DIRTY

SAD

AUTUMN

SMALL

LOUD

544. Identify and place the gender nouns in the correct columns.

Daughter   Son   Gentleman   Mother
Horse   Mare   Queen   Aunt
Father   Uncle   Niece   Nephew

Feminine	Masculine

545. Choose the correct nouns to complete the following sentences.

1. The _____ is made of wood.

i. Chair   ii. Jacket   iii. Clay

2. I wore a pretty _____.

i. Candle   ii. Door   iii. Dress

3. It's very hot. Could you please switch on the _____?

i. Fan   ii. Leaves   iii. Geyser

4. The king wears a _____ on his head.

i. Throne   ii. Crown   iii. Castle

546. Complete the sentences using the correct opposites.

Happy   Hot   Mouse   Shut

The tea is _____, but the juice is cold.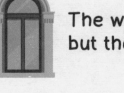

 The window is _____, but the door is open.

An elephant is big, but a _____ is small.

Honey is _____, but Sheena is sad.

547. Complete the sentences below using a/an.

1. This is _____ bat.

2. This is _____ apple.

3. That is _____ boat.

4. This is _____ astronaut.

5. This is _____ fish.

6. She has _____ idea.

7. My mother is _____ cook.

8. My friend has _____ dog.

548. Choose the correct option and complete the sentences.

1. The wind _____ (blue / blew) the leaves.

2. I'll _____ (meet / meat) my friend today.

3. Can we go to the _____ (fair / fare) today?

4. I have _____ (scene / seen) the movie.

5. Is that a _____ (bee / be) on the flower?

549. Solve the crossword puzzle using picture clues.

550. Fill in the blanks with the correct forms of nouns.

1. There are uncountable _____ (star / stars) in the sky.

2. Will you be taking the _____? (stairs / stair)

3. Kevin's favorite _____ (book / books) is *The Happy Prince*.

4. John has a brown _____. (dogs / dog)

5. A rainbow has seven _____. (colors / color)

6. The _____ (cats / cat) is sitting on the table.

551. List 8 things that you see in the given image.

552. Write 5 sentences about your school.

_____

_____

_____

_____

_____

_____

_____

_____

_____

_____

553. Which is your favorite subject and why?

554. Who is your best friend in school. Write 2 lines to describe them.

555. Who is your favorite teacher and why?